Petrarch's Penitential Psalms and Prayers

THE WILLIAM AND KATHERINE DEVERS SERIES IN DANTE AND MEDIEVAL ITALIAN LITERATURE

Zygmunt G. Barański, Theodore J. Cachey, Jr., and Christian Moevs, *editors*

RECENT TITLES

VOLUME 24
Petrarch's Penitential Psalms and Prayers
• Francesco Petrarca, edited and translated by Demetrio S. Yocum

VOLUME 23
Dante's "Vita Nova": A Collaborative Reading
• Edited by Zygmunt G. Barański and Heather Webb

VOLUME 22
Manuscript Poetics: Materiality and Textuality in Medieval Italian Literature
• Francesco Marco Aresu

VOLUME 21
Dante's Multitudes: History, Philosophy, Method
• Teodolinda Barolini

VOLUME 20
Dante's "Other Works": Assessments and Interpretations
• Edited by Zygmunt G. Barański and Theodore J. Cachey, Jr.

VOLUME 19
Liturgical Song and Practice in Dante's Commedia
• Helena Phillips-Robins

VOLUME 18
Dante and Violence: Domestic, Civic, and Cosmic
• Brenda Deen Schildgen

VOLUME 17
A Boccaccian Renaissance: Essays on the Early Modern Impact of Giovanni Boccaccio and His Works
• Edited by Martin Eisner and David Lummus

VOLUME 16
The Portrait of Beatrice: Dante, D. G. Rossetti, and the Imaginary Lady
• Fabio A. Camilletti

VOLUME 15
Boccaccio's Corpus: Allegory, Ethics, and Vernacularity
• James C. Kriesel

VOLUME 14
Meditations on the Life of Christ: The Short Italian Text
• Sarah McNamer

VOLUME 13
Interpreting Dante: Essays on the Traditions of Dante Commentary
• Edited by Paola Nasti and Claudia Rossignoli

VOLUME 12
Freedom Readers: The African American Reception of Dante Alighieri and the Divine Comedy
• Dennis Looney

VOLUME 11
Dante's Commedia: *Theology as Poetry*
• Edited by Vittorio Montemaggi and Matthew Treherne

VOLUME 10
Petrarch and Dante: Anti-Dantism, Metaphysics, Tradition
• Edited by Zygmunt G. Barański and Theodore J. Cachey, Jr.

VOLUME 9
The Ancient Flame: Dante and the Poets
• Winthrop Wetherbee

VOLUME 8
Accounting for Dante: Urban Readers and Writers in Late Medieval Italy
• Justin Steinberg

VOLUME 7
Experiencing the Afterlife: Soul and Body in Dante and Medieval Culture
• Manuele Gragnolati

VOLUME 6
Understanding Dante
• John A. Scott

VOLUME 5
Dante and the Grammar of the Nursing Body
• Gary P. Cestaro

VOLUME 4
The Fiore *and the* Detto d'Amore: *A Late 13th-Century Italian Translation of the* Roman de la Rose, *Attributable to Dante*
• Translated, with introduction and notes, by Santa Casciani and Christopher Kleinhenz

Winner of the 2023 Aldo and Jeanne Scaglione Publication Award for a Manuscript in Italian Literary Studies, Modern Language Association

PETRARCH'S PENITENTIAL PSALMS AND PRAYERS

FRANCESCO PETRARCA

Edited and translated by Demetrio S. Yocum

University of Notre Dame Press
Notre Dame, Indiana

Copyright © 2024 by the University of Notre Dame

Published by the University of Notre Dame Press
Notre Dame, Indiana 46556
undpress.nd.edu

All Rights Reserved

Published in the United States of America

Library of Congress Control Number: 2023946558

ISBN: 978-0-268-20784-7 (Hardback)
ISBN: 978-0-268-20785-4 (Paperback)
ISBN: 978-0-268-20788-5 (WebPDF)
ISBN: 978-0-268-20783-0 (Epub)

ABOUT THE WILLIAM AND KATHERINE
DEVERS SERIES IN DANTE AND
MEDIEVAL ITALIAN LITERATURE

The William and Katherine Devers Program in Dante Studies at the University of Notre Dame supports rare book acquisitions in the university's John A. Zahm Dante collections, funds a visiting professorship in Dante studies, and supports electronic and print publication of scholarly research in the field. In collaboration with the Medieval Institute at the university, the Devers program initiated a series dedicated to the publication of the most significant current scholarship in the field of Dante studies. In 2011 the scope of the series was expanded to encompass thirteenth- and fourteenth-century Italian literature.

In keeping with the spirit that inspired the creation of the Devers program, the series takes Dante and medieval Italian literature as focal points that draw together the many disciplines and lines of inquiry that constitute a cultural tradition without fixed boundaries. Accordingly, the series hopes to illuminate this cultural tradition within contemporary critical debates in the humanities by reflecting both the highest quality of scholarly achievement and the greatest diversity of critical perspectives.

The series publishes works from a wide variety of disciplinary viewpoints and in diverse scholarly genres, including critical studies, commentaries, editions, reception studies, translations, and conference proceedings of exceptional importance. The series enjoys the support of an international advisory board composed of distinguished scholars and is published regularly by the University of Notre Dame Press. The Dolphin and Anchor device that appears on publications of the Devers series was used by the great humanist, grammarian, editor, and typographer Aldus Manutius (1449–1515), in whose 1502 edition of Dante (second issue) and all subsequent editions it appeared. The device illustrates the ancient proverb Festina lente, "Hurry up slowly."

Zygmunt G. Barański, Theodore J. Cachey, Jr.,
and Christian Moevs, *editors*

ADVISORY BOARD

Albert Russell Ascoli, Berkeley

Teodolinda Barolini, Columbia

Piero Boitani, Rome

Patrick Boyde, Cambridge

Alison Cornish, New York University

Christopher Kleinhenz, Wisconsin

Giuseppe Ledda, Bologna

Simone Marchesi, Princeton

Kristina M. Olson, George Mason

Lino Pertile, Harvard

John A. Scott, Western Australia

Heather Webb, Cambridge

For my parents, Lina and David, and my spouse, Nathan

CONTENTS

Acknowledgments ... xi

Conventions and Abbreviations ... xv

Introduction ... xvii
   Notes to Introduction ... xli

A Note on the Translation ... lxi

Petrarch's Seven Psalms ... 1
   Notes to Psalms ... 20

Petrarch's Prayers ... 49
   Notes to Prayers ... 62

Bibliography ... 67

Index of References and Passages from Petrarch's Works ... 79

Index of Scriptural References ... 83

General Index ... 87

ACKNOWLEDGMENTS

Petrarch's *devotiuncula* has passed down the centuries as a "penitential" poetic composition, and I must confess that I have experienced moments when writing the present work, which has taken about seven years—seven is also the number of the traditional penitential psalms as well as those authored by Petrarch—to complete, felt like a penance of sorts more than anything else. However, the ability to express here and now my profound gratitude for the support of colleagues, friends, and family represents a moment of great joy and delight worth all the long hours and hard work.

Throughout the time spent writing this work, I had the benefit of unwavering support and encouragement from colleagues and students in Italian Studies at the University of Notre Dame. I am especially thankful to Ted Cachey and Zyg Barański, who have been very supportive of my research over the years. They offered thoughtful comments and astute criticisms that allowed me to significantly improve the quality of the whole work. I also owe a deep debt of gratitude to David Lummus, a very fine Latinist, who supported the project and painstakingly reviewed and corrected my translation in its earliest stages. I also benefited from participating in Ted's Petrarch: Poetry in Motion course in fall 2018; the graduate students' brilliant presentations, questions, and comments led me to see aspects of Petrarch's works more clearly and in new perspectives. I wish to thank in particular Mattia Boccuti, who during that course presented on Petrarch's psalms and later shared with me an earlier version of his article on the topic.

At Notre Dame, I also wish to thank most warmly Jean Porter and the late Joe Blenkinsopp for their friendship and sparkling conversation over many lovely dinners. On various occasions, Joe, a preeminent scholar of Isaiah but also a devoted lover of Italian language and literature, clarified for me many aspects of the book of Psalms and the religious life of ancient

Israel—when not reciting by heart verses from Dante and Leopardi. I would also like to express my gratitude to Kathleen and Tom Cummings for their support and friendship throughout the years.

Over these past several years I also received support and advice from friends and colleagues at other institutions—on both sides of the Atlantic. Heartfelt thanks go to Wanda Balzano and Jefferson Holdridge at Wake Forest for their irreplaceable friendship and for reading a later version of my work. As poets and Latinists in their own right, they provided many valuable insights that helped render my English translation more fluent and expressive. I am very grateful to Raymond Studzinski at Catholic University for his friendship over the years, for reading earlier versions of my translation, and for offering sage advice. I received valuable insights and clarifications on the Hebrew Psalter and Jerome's Latin translations from Michael Graves of Wheaton College. Paolo Squillacioti at the Opera del Vocabolario Italiano in Florence has offered support and has been a source of inspiration and motivation over the years. Writing during the pandemic has presented a variety of challenges, and I would like to thank most warmly Tiziana Terranova for her friendship and constant support in the darkest hours. Special thanks go also to Giuseppe Balirano, Kim Belcher, Mattias Bürghel, Jacques Dupont, Tommaso Guadagno, Steve Molvarec, Vittorio Ruggiero, and Marianna Starita for their steadfast encouragement, friendship, warmth, and sense of humor.

At Saint Mary's College, I would like to thank in particular Umberto Taccheri and Jennifer Zachman and all my other colleagues in the Department of Modern Languages, including Pamela Hardig, administrative assistant, and my students, who, especially during the pandemic, helped me keep in good spirits with their wit, intellectual exchange, and fruitful conversation.

My research for this book benefited from the friendship and professional assistance of Tracy Bergstrom, former Director of Specialized Collection Services at Hesburgh Library at Notre Dame, who has always been available to offer expert advice and assistance.

I am very grateful to the professional and courteous acquisitions, editorial, and production teams at the University of Notre Dame Press. I wish to thank in particular Sheila Berg, Matt Dowd, Megan Levine, Stephanie Marchman, Wendy McMillen, and Laura Moran Walton. Their dedication, expertise, and attention to detail were instrumental in bringing this project to fruition. Special thanks go also to the two reviewers whose detailed comments and excellent suggestions much improved the work. Any errors that remain, however, are my responsibility alone.

I want to express my warmest thanks to Vincenzo Fera, President of the National Commission for the Works of Francesco Petrarca; Donatella Coppini; and the members of the National Commission and Casa Editrice Le Lettere of Florence for allowing me to reproduce the Latin text of Petrarch's psalms and prayers edited by Donatella Coppini for the series *Petrarca del centenario*.

I am very grateful to the MLA selection committee—Kevin Brownlee, Marilyn Migiel, Dana Renga, and Barbara Spackman—who have named my manuscript winner of the 2023 Aldo Scaglione Publication Award for a Manuscript in Italian Literary Studies.

Many thanks are also due to my sister, Mariolina; my brothers, Dario and Davide; my nieces, Claire, Marika, and Molly; my great-nieces, Kristen and Bailey; and my great-nephews, Dillan and Jayden, for their constant love and support.

I would be remiss if I did not recognize the many feline companions, Guigo, Walt, Cicci, Bella, Leo, and Felix, among others, who over the years made writing this work so much more enjoyable. If Petrarch's embalmed cat still proclaims from the epitaph on her tomb at Arquà that she was "the greater of his [Petrarch's] flames, Laura was the second," there is certainly a good reason for that.

Finally, I dedicate this book to the loving memory of my parents, Lina and David, for their unconditional love and support and for always encouraging and believing in me, and to my dear spouse, Nathan, who has been by my side for twenty wonderful years, for his insight, patience, humor, and support throughout.

> *Even with subdued, weak voices God's majesty is honored. For if only the spirit resounds, there is such a cry to him that he himself hears it in heaven.*
>
> —Bach, Cantata BWV 36. 7 Aria (Soprano) "Auch mit gedämpften, schwachen Stimmen"

CONVENTIONS AND ABBREVIATIONS

All quotations from the Vulgate Bible are taken from *Biblia Sacra Vulgata: Editio quinta*, edited by Robert Weber and Roger Gryson: https://www.academic-bible.com/en/bible-society-and-biblical-studies/scholarly-editions/vulgate/.

English translations of all Latin Vulgate Bible texts are from the *New Revised Standard Version Updated Edition* (NRSVUE): https://www.biblegateway.com/versions/New-Revised-Standard-Version-Updated-Edition-NRSVue-Bible/.

Psalms with a capital *P* indicate the 150 poems in the book of Psalms; when I refer to Petrarch's psalms, I use a lowercase *p*.

References to the Psalms are according to the Septuagint-Vulgate numbering scheme, followed, when necessary, in parenthesis by the Hebrew numbering scheme, which is the version used by most modern editions of the Bible.

Unless otherwise noted, all translations from Latin and Italian are my own. Whenever I have modified the wording of a published translation, mainly for clarity, nuance, and inclusiveness, I have indicated it in the notes.

Petrarch's sources in Latin, Italian, and English, with their abbreviated titles and translations, are as follows:

Dor.	*De otio religioso* (Latin, ed. Goletti); *On Religious Leisure* (trans. Schearer).
Dvs.	*De vita solitaria* (Latin, ed. Martellotti); *The Life of Solitude* (trans. Zeitlin).
Ep. Metr.	*Epistulae metricae* (Latin, ed. Otto Schönberger)

Fam.	*Familiares. Rerum familiarum libri*; *Le familiari* (Latin, ed. Rossi and Bosco); *Letters on Familiar Matters* (trans. Bernardo et al.).
Rvf.	*Rerum vulgarium fragmenta*; *Canzoniere* (Italian, ed. Santagata); *Petrarch's Lyric Poems* (trans. Durling).
Secretum	*Secretum. De secretu conflictu curarum mearum*; *Il mio segreto* (Latin, ed. Fenzi); *My Secret Book* (ed. and trans. Mann).
Sen.	*Seniles. Rerum senilium libri*; *Le senili* (Latin, ed. Rizzo and Berté); *Letters of Old Age* (trans. Bernardo et al.).

The following abbreviations have also been adopted throughout:

CC	Corpus Corporum: repositorium operum Latinorum apud universitatem Turicensem, https://mlat.uzh.ch/.
PL	Patrologiae Cursus Completus, Series Latina.

INTRODUCTION

In Petrarch's last letter to his brother Gherardo, who earlier in life had abandoned his literary ambitions to become a Carthusian monk, most likely written in spring 1372, that is, two years before his death, Petrarch describes how he spends his time at Arquà: "always reading and writing and praising God."[1] These carefully chosen words seem almost intended to reassure Gherardo of the fact that, at last, his older, more restless brother had finally found, in the world outside monastic cloister walls, the peace and quiet of a "modest, and solitary life" similar to his own at the charterhouse of Montrieux.[2]

In effect, these three activities, which may be considered the essence of monastic life, were essentially Petrarch's ordinary, constant occupations and sum up well his entire life. Interestingly, Petrarch lists these activities one after the other in close succession. However, from what we know of Petrarch's life and work, reading, writing, and praising God were deeply intertwined, with the praise of God often perceived as the loftiest goal and often pervading the other two.[3] As a cleric with minor orders, who took the recitation of the Divine Office seriously, this should hardly come as a surprise. The same testament, written later in life, confirms the importance Petrarch attached to the bequeathing of his breviaries.[4] Even at the time of his more overt and active political engagement—his support of Cola di Rienzo's failed coup of 1347 comes immediately to mind—and pursuit of worldly ambitions such as fame and glory—epitomized by his crowning as poet laureate—there is always a clear emphasis on the ultimate good and on God as worthy of praise.[5] This awareness emerges most clearly on the occasion of Petrarch's acceptance of the laurel crown as poet in Rome, on the Capitoline on Easter Sunday, April 8, 1341. In his coronation oration, despite the overall focus on and references to the role of the poet and poetry in classical Latin authors, God is ultimately praised as the giver and bestower of his poetic genius.[6]

If the praise of God is expressed on numerous occasions and in many forms throughout Petrarch's writings, the expression "Deum laudans" in *Sen.* 15.5 may well imply the reciting of the Divine Office, traditionally referred to as the liturgy of the hours, or *Opus Dei*.[7] As a cleric, Petrarch was in fact very familiar with reciting the Divine Office, which since early Christianity had been considered part of the official and public worship of the church, thereby continuing a long-established Jewish tradition of reciting prayers and psalms at certain hours of the day and night.[8] This is confirmed by the fact that Petrarch owned two breviaries, liturgical books containing the canonical hymns, prayers, and Psalms for daily use, one of which, it would seem, has come down to us.[9] In several letters Petrarch mentions his time spent reciting the Divine Office, and in one of his letters to Gherardo he would specifically write that he now heeds his advice not only in avoiding women and confessing his sins but also in rising at night to pray the Divine Office.[10]

Petrarch was, therefore, very familiar with the Psalms, which still to this day constitute the backbone of the liturgy of the hours.[11] Although this included other prayers, antiphons, versicles, and readings, depending on the various liturgical seasons, the reciting, or singing, of the Psalms was unquestionably the main component of the Divine Office. As part of the daily readings and devotions of Christians throughout Western Europe in the Middle Ages, thanks to the increasing circulation and production of books of hours—smaller in format and portable—the Psalms had a profound and lasting impact on European culture, spirituality, faith, and literary production.[12]

Not surprisingly, Psalms is among the most cited (if not the most cited) book in Petrarch's writings.[13] In his letter to Francesco Nelli—who may have provided Petrarch with his second, portable breviary—he would write that he desires "to have his [David's] Psalter always at hand and within sight while awake and beneath my pillow while sleeping and at point of death."[14] Years later, and perhaps more powerfully, he would express the same thought in his last letter to Gherardo cited earlier (*Sen.* 15.5). Writing about how he is "praying incessantly to Christ for a good end of life and for His mercy and forgiveness," he adds, "There is nothing that sounds sweeter on my lips than those words of David, 'Do not remember the sins of my youth and my follies' [Ps. 25.7]."[15] Earlier, in another important letter to Gherardo, he wrote, "As for the Psalms, undoubtedly you are following the advice of Jerome, that they never slip from your hands. . . . [D]ivide all your life between contemplation and psalm singing and homilies and readings."[16]

But it is in the two "twin" Latin treatises, *De vita solitaria* (hereafter *Dvs.*) and *De otio religioso* (hereafter *Dor.*), as Petrarch himself referred to them, that the Psalms are explored more fully in their spiritual and liturgical sense and become central to the overall structure of both texts. In the first chapter of *Dvs.*, in fact, Petrarch describes the daily life—most likely mirroring his own at Vaucluse—of a solitary country dweller devoted to reading and writing and whose day is regulated by reciting the office seven times a day, according to the Christian liturgical tradition. Moreover, each hour of the sevenfold recitation of the office, is evoked by referring to the traditional liturgical hymns sung before the psalms prescribed for the office of the day.[17]

In similar fashion, in the prologue of *Dor.*, the treatise written during Lent 1347 and dedicated to his brother and the Carthusians, Petrarch's first direct observation of his stay with the community documents the Carthusians' "angelicam psalmodiam" (angelic singing of the Psalms).[18] The treatise ends with Petrarch recalling his supposedly late conversion to scripture and the ensuing dedication to celebrating the Divine Office, thus, to "reflect upon David's Psalms, a source from which I have been eager to drink, not that I might become a more learned man, but a better one, if I could, nor that I could come out of it a better dialectician, but a less corrupt sinner."[19] More importantly, the entire treatise is structured on Psalm 45.11 (46.10), *Vacate et videte quoniam ego sum Deus* (Be still and know that I am God), and throughout the text these verses are recited and "ruminated" over and over again, not only as a reminder against the temptations of the world, but also as the only way to experience God's presence. Thus, in adopting the traditional monastic practice of reading and praying, traditionally referred to as *lectio divina*, Petrarch confirms his interest in reproducing, better yet, providing, a new inflected idiom, a monastic "style" centered on scriptural-patristic exegesis and affective devotional practices.[20]

Petrarch's familiarity with and interest in the Psalms, however, was not merely confined to his liturgical or devotional practices. He also regarded the Davidic Psalms as an important poetic model rivaling the classical poetry of Homer and Virgil and worthy of imitation for their "dulcore latenti" (mysterious sweetness) that "penetrans . . . animos" (reaches into souls).[21] Although Petrarch stresses, in *Fam.* 10.4.31, David's somewhat unenticing "vox rauca" (hoarse voice) caused by the "lacrimarum assiduitas" (unceasing tears) and the psalmic "asperum" (rough) and "flebilem" (mournful, tearful) style, he will closely associate it with a monastic character that clearly pervades several of his writings.[22]

It is precisely this monastic-liturgical style, combined with his unique personal, classical, humanist, and elegiac voice, that will characterize Petrarch's seven psalms. Thanks to their experimental originality, these compositions present elements of the poem-prayers of the *Rerum vulgarium fragmenta* (hereafter *Rvf.*), the poems in praise of Mary Magdalene (*Carmen de Magdalena*), and the liturgical prayers that Petrarch wrote in the course of his life, which are included in the present volume as well.[23]

As equally elaborate poetic compositions and paraliturgical, devotional texts, Petrarch's psalms represent, despite the scant scholarly attention that they have received over the years, an important intellectual achievement in the wider context of Petrarch's oeuvre, one that reminds us of Petrarch's complex cultural project, a project that never saw him shy away from engaging in worldly and political affairs, yet one that often meant positioning himself at a safe, quasi-monastic distance from which he could then meticulously craft the image of himself not only as civic poet and public intellectual but also as religious, spiritual *auctor*.[24] If in fact recent valuable studies have cogently pointed to Petrarch's views of the role of the poet, and his defense of poetry, as means to establish his authority in political and civic contexts, his religious treatises and his psalms and prayers—most likely written around the same time of Cola di Rienzo's failed coup—remind us that his reach was also intended to go beyond the strictly political sphere in order to assert his authority as moral guide and religious writer.

Moreover, on the basis of his new, humanist understanding of the self and its relationship with God, Petrarch in several of his writings will deliberately engage in conversation, if not openly challenge, the church's traditional—and mostly immutable—doctrine and teachings through a more complex, and less univocal, approach to human experience, knowledge, and faith. His attempt to assert his intellectual authority by disaffiliating himself from a certain type of worldly *negotium* and, at the same time, by claiming his autonomy from institutionalized forms of ecclesial power may also be considered one of the first modern attempts to redefine contemplative withdrawal (characteristic of the monastic medieval tradition) as an act of political dissent and intellectual resistance. To put it simply, Petrarch the humanist, civic poet and Petrarch the Christian, religious writer are one and the same.

The Psalms in Petrarch's Life and Oeuvre

As with many of his works, which were subject to constant revisions and rewritings over prolonged periods and throughout the course of his life, the dating of Petrarch's psalms is still debated, though the current scholarly consensus is that they were most likely written sometime between 1343 and 1350, with strong arguments for 1348.[25] The 1340s and early 1350s were, in effect, the most consequential in Petrarch's life and crucial for his literary output. During this time, we witness Petrarch's gradual distancing from Avignon's papal curia and the abandonment of "transalpina solitudo mea jocundissima" (my most delightful transalpine solitude) at Vaucluse to his relocation in northern Italy, first at Parma, as archdeacon, and then Milan, where he moved after being called by the Viscontis in 1353. During these years, Petrarch also distances himself from his more classically inspired works in Latin, mainly left unfinished, and the beginning of works clearly inspired by his patristic readings—first and foremost, Augustine—and more oriented to autobiography, self-knowledge, and introspection, on the one hand, and Christian ethics and spirituality, on the other. A case could be made that after his coronation as poet laureate in Rome in 1341, Petrarch was left with the realization that worldly pursuits such as fame and glory and the crafting of the image of himself for posterity as the direct heir of the great classical Latin tradition conflicted with his moral and spiritual aspirations, a conflict (or sense of guilt?) that may have characterized his entire life.

These conflicting aspirations were most likely triggered by several unexpected and mostly grief-stricken events in his life. Along with the death—

caused by the plague in 1348—of many dear friends, including his beloved Laura, his political ambitions were thwarted by the demise of Cola di Rienzo in Rome.[26] Another major event that would have profound repercussions at this time on Petrarch's life and work was his brother Gherardo's decision to withdraw from the world and join the Carthusian order in 1343.[27] It is in fact to a monastic, or perhaps Carthusian, ideal that Petrarch would turn to fashion the image of himself as focused on a life of solitude and lofty literary pursuits and to create, for his contemporary readers and posterity, an image of himself as spiritual and moral *auctoritas*. However, as noted earlier, this distancing of himself from worldly matters did not entail a complete detachment from worldly affairs.[28]

It is not surprising, therefore, that scholars have viewed Petrarch's *devotiuncula*, as he himself referred to his psalms in a letter of 1371 to Francesco Bruni, thus revealing the work's primary devotional function, as chronologically, and ideally, close to several of Petrarch's more religious texts such as *Dvs.* (1346), *Dor.* (1347), and the *Secretum* (1347, 1349, and 1353).[29] It is in these Latin treatises, in fact, that Petrarch adopts and adapts a "monastic" style, which he explicitly mentions for the first time in one of his letters to Gherardo, a "style" based primarily on affective, spiritual readings, themes, and practices.[30] Moreover, in these works Petrarch will often stage his inner conflicts and subtly compare his wayward life choices to those of his brother, who, unlike him, was "able to scorn the world" and abandon the "fancy words" of poetry "sung in a popular manner"[31] to follow his call to become a monk, or, as expressed in his letter on Mount Ventoux, to climb "the most direct path" to the ultimate summit.[32] Indeed, the contrast between the two brothers' destiny as religious, one under the austere Carthusian rule, the other as an ordinary cleric with minor orders, is seen by Petrarch through the lens of Psalm 123.8 (124.8): "what other reason can it be if not that, our bonds having been equally broken, what followed was unequal: 'our help in the name of the Lord'? Why have we concluded in such discord this Davidic Psalm begun in such harmony?"[33]

Although Petrarch ultimately rejects a call to join his brother as a Carthusian monk, it is on this moral predicament, or *dissidio*, between a monastic life, dedicated to contemplation and writing religious works, and one focused instead on more worldly literary pursuits that he will devise a laicized version of the monastic ideal and create a new image of himself as a moral and spiritual *auctoritas*. Inspired primarily by Augustine's *Confessions*, Petrarch in several of his works of this period—in particular, *Dvs.*, *Dor.*, and above all the *Secretum*—lays bare spiritual and moral dilemmas while also making the radical confession of shortfalls and sinfulness, just as the bishop of Hippo had done many centuries earlier. In the specific case of his psalms, Petrarch rewrites the Davidic Psalms to create poetic compositions that, on the one hand, invoke God directly and reveal the sinfulness and *miseria* of the poet-penitent and, on the other, represent a deliberate attempt to redefine and put his own classical, humanist mark on a traditional devotional genre.[34]

Petrarch's religious turn has often been met with a certain dose of skepticism among some scholars. However, whether Petrarch's psalms were a form of exomologesis, or another poetic strategy to establish his authority particularly in religious and monastic circles, or perhaps a shrouded attempt at achieving fame and glory under spiritual pretenses is beyond the scope of this study. What we can attest instead is the presence of autobiographical elements, inspired by or modeled on Augustine's *Confessions* and consistent with his other "monastic" works of the same period, which bring to light a more profound reflection on personal, spiritual matters.

Another unquestionable fact is that Petrarch's seven psalms circulated widely, particularly in monastic settings, along with other devotional and paraliturgical texts.[35] If today we are more inclined to see them as creative spiritual expressions somewhere between poetry and prayer, during the time of their first circulation, the manuscript tradition confirms that they were unmistakably considered quasi-liturgical prayers, almost on a par with the Davidic Psalms, and, as such, they were read, recited, even chanted in various religious settings.[36]

The closest description left by Petrarch of his psalms is in *Sen.* 10.1, a letter written to his friend Sagremor de Pommiers, upon the latter's entrance into the Cistercian order.

> I sent the seven psalms that I long ago composed for myself in my misery. I wish they were as edifying as they are inelegant. . . . You will read them as they are and do so more patiently if you will remember that they are what you asked for, and that I dictated them many years ago in less than one day.[37]

Petrarch writes that he composed the psalms "long ago," "for himself," and at a time of "misery."[38] More importantly for our purposes, Petrarch defines them "as edifying as they are inelegant," thus shedding light on his careful attempt to create a poetic linguistic style characterized by *inculte* (inelegant), plain, rhythmic, prose-like verses, a style reminiscent of Jerome's own rendering in Latin of the Davidic Psalms.

Like most psalters and other types of prayer books in the Middle Ages, Petrarch's Roman breviary, and the version of Psalms he most likely knew, employed the standard "Vulgate" Psalter, that is, Jerome's so-called Gallican Psalter, which became the official, standard Psalter of medieval Western Europe. The Gallican Psalter, so called because it became dominant in Gaul (when Alcuin preferred it to Jerome's Hebrew version for the edition of the Bible he presented to Charlemagne in the early ninth century), was Jerome's second attempt at translating the Psalms. His first attempt was mainly a cursory revision of the *Vetus Latina* version; for the second attempt, he instead relied on Origen's Hexaplaric Septuagint, not in the original Hebrew; and for the third, he followed the Hebrew text. Compared to the *Vetus Latina* version, the Gallican Psalter is still a word-for-word translation but more idiomatic.[39] Jerome was well trained in the classics and a master of Latin style. Although he kept a conservative approach and tended to give a literal translation, like the *Vetus Latina*, for the Gallican, he also wanted the Latin to be stylistically adequate and idiomatically correct. As a result, Jerome's Latin translation is neither classical poetry nor prose.[40]

It is in *Parthenias*, the first eclogue of the *Bucolicum carmen*, composed in 1347, and then in the explanatory letter to Gherardo, *Fam.* 10.4 (1349), sent together to Gherardo, that Petrarch offers what scholars consider his most systematic reflection on poetry and its relation to theology and truth. The latter is defined in the first part of the letter as "the poetry of God," and the Davidic Psalms, the ones that "quod die noctuque canitis" (you [Gherardo] sing day and night), are offered as an important poetic model as they "apud Hebreos metro constat" (possess poetic meter in Hebrew), while David is called "Cristianorum poetam" (poet of the Christians).[41] More significantly, Petrarch notes that Jerome's Latin translations were able not only to reproduce its meaning but also to preserve "nescioquid . . . metrice legis," a metrical quality that allows us to call those lines of the Psalms verses.[42] In the following section of the letter, Petrarch offers a defense of style according to which both poetry and theology, based on their common, intrinsic nature, are conducive to truth, albeit their different styles "concentrate on the meaning; if it is true and wholesome, embrace it regardless of the style."⁴³

Parthenias is a dialogue between two shepherds, Monicus (Gherardo), who lives withdrawn from society in a cave (Montrieux, Gherardo's Carthusian monastery) and listens to David's Psalms sung during the liturgy, and Silvius (Petrarch), whose aspiration to write poetry leads him to "go straying o'er thorny hills" (v. 3) and follow the two noble and generous shepherds Virgil and Homer. Monicus then invites Silvius to abandon his wanderings and enter the cave, where "in the depths of night, you will see a shepherd tuning / Notes of unrivalled sweetness, to make you in time forgetful / Heedless of all other matters" (vv. 55–56). But Silvius declines the invitation in the end: "Love of the Muse compels me" (v. 112). Thus he returns to the writing of the *Africa*, ending, somewhat abruptly, the dialogue.⁴⁴

The eclogue and *Fam.* 10.4 are Petrarch's most exhaustive reflection on the two types of poetry, the classical and the Davidic. Moreover, if the two brothers' separate paths could be seen as representations of Petrarch's inner tension between withdrawal from the world—the singing of Psalms—and engagement with it—reconciling through poetry classical culture and Christian faith—he ultimately articulates a defense of both, with David's Psalms presented as "hoarse" but "sweet." Yet the classical poetry of his champions Virgil and Homer is the one he will keep pursuing—for the time being. If in fact the dialogue is interrupted by Silvius-Petrarch returning to the composition of the *Africa*, he would eventually adopt the Davidic "flebilem" (tearful) style to write his own psalms.⁴⁵

What the dialogue between the two shepherds ultimately sheds light on is that if, on the one hand, the inner conflicts between secular and religious life—or between Petrarch's more tentative, worldly life choices compared to Gherardo's unfaltering withdrawal from the world—may have never completely abandoned Petrarch during his life, on the other hand, they found resolution in his writing. Throughout his works, in fact, there emerges a clear intent to set side by side the simple and *inculte* (inelegant) style of the Psalms and scripture and the refined, elegant style of his classical *auctores*. If at times throughout his writings and letters Petrarch seems to engage in a rhetorical defense of the latter or present the two as somewhat antithetical—just as his champions Augustine and Jerome had done earlier⁴⁶—the continuity

xxvi Introduction

between classical and Christian culture was an unwavering truth for Petrarch, one that underpins his Christian humanism.[47] Never does Petrarch question the validity of classical teachings for the growth and well-being of the human mind and spirit if rightly applied and interpreted according to Christian doctrine: both are worth pursuing; both are conducive to salvation.[48]

CHRISTIAN AND CLASSICAL SOURCES

Attempts at rewriting, translating, paraphrasing, and versifying scripture in general and psalms in particular were not original to Petrarch.[49] Although his psalms provided a first and unique model that was later imitated by numerous authors, mainly in the vernacular, Petrarch's psalms should be seen in a much larger context of Christian liturgical, paraliturgical, and devotional literature that had circulated widely since the fourth century and that was either based on scripture or inspired by it.[50] Petrarch's *devotiuncula* is also part of the apparent growth of private piety in the late Middle Ages and is closely related to the development of silent reading, which grew exponentially with the rise of portable books of prayers.[51]

Already Latin Christian poets of late antiquity, following the lesson of classical rhetorical schools and expert orators trained in the exercise of paraphrase, had begun to versify biblical narrative according to a variety of stylistic procedures and for diverse purposes.[52] Christian paraphrasts followed the exegetical methods of the church fathers, and for them *imitatio* and biblical versification were didactic, with the main goal being to offer moral and doctrinal commentary without altering the biblical message. On the other hand, these were clearly intended as an ascetic and devotional practice intended to nourish the soul and to prolong prayer and contemplation while being engaged in the act of writing.

Petrarch was familiar with many of the late Latin Christian authors and mentions several of them in *Fam.* 10.4 (after giving precedence to those he calls "duces," or authorities, namely, Ambrose, Augustine, and Jerome) as having "made use of poetry and rhythm": Prudentius, Prosper of Aquitaine, and Sedulius, of whom "we have none of their prose and only a few works in verse."[53] A more detailed account of these early Latin versifiers is offered in the tenth eclogue of the *Bucolicum carmen* in a section where, in keeping with the eclogues' overall agricultural metaphor, Arator, Prudentius, Sedulius, and Juvencus are seen as cultivators of poetry who, however, despite the fertility of the land, are unable to grow a "laurel" or "any green for a garland" because their "voices were weak," a clear reference to their inadequate poetic style.[54]

If the late Latin Christian poets are deemed inadequate as *auctoritates*, Petrarch's psalms reveal a clear indebtedness to the classical authors he championed throughout his life: Cicero, Horace, Ovid, and others, as several scholars have pointed out.[55] However, the allusions and references to these models are distinctly filtered through a Christian understanding of life—with all its joys and sorrows—death, and salvation. The overlapping of citations and topoi from the classical *auctores* is a constant in Petrarch's oeuvre, where the convergence of classical, patristic, and scriptural sources points to his central belief in the universal nature of humankind's deepest aspirations, ideals, and torments. It is on the basis of a dignified view of the human condition that Petrarch can envision the continuity between classical culture and Christian knowledge, thus opening the door to humanist studies and the Renaissance.

A closely related poetic genre with which Petrarch was very familiar was Christian Latin hymnody. The earliest Latin hymns, influenced by the Eastern hymnodic tradition, can be traced as far back as the fourth century.[56] Hymns started to be incorporated in the Christian mass and Benedictine liturgy from the sixth century on, and a significant development in hymn production and diversification came with the development of the Divine Office. Alongside the various hymnodic compositions incorporated in the mass and liturgical worship (tropes, sequences, versus), we find paraliturgical (*rondelli*, motets) and nonliturgical compositions like the *pia dictamina* (or *rhythmi*) that became widespread throughout Europe starting in the eleventh century. *Pia dictamina*, which were meditative, panegyric, rhythmically structured hymns intended for private meditation and at times accompanied by melodies, are of particular interest as their popularity increased in the fourteenth century. Drawing on various sources, such as the Bible, sermons, commentaries, and legends, these hymns include elaborate and lengthy versified rosaries (with fifty strophes for the fifty Hail Marys of the Rosary), sets of *officia parva*, and rhythmic psalters with 150 strophes mostly centered on Christ or Mary.[57] The popularity of the *pia dictamina* is without a doubt linked to the emergence of new forms and expressions of secular devotion across Europe (in particular, the *devotio moderna* movement), including new forms of meditative practices that originated in reformed monastic orders like the Carthusian. Their diffusion was also the result of the ever-widening circulation and production of prayer books and, later, books of hours and breviaries.

Milan was the center of Ambrosian (and pseudo-Ambrosian) hymnody, which Petrarch knew well, as hymns were included in most breviaries and books of hours of the time. The first Petrarchan attempt at devotional paraphrase, through the typical techniques of transposition, amplification, and abbreviation, can be seen in *Dvs.*, where, as noted earlier, a prose rendition of Ambrosian hymns is central to the prologue describing the solitary life of the country dweller regulated by the daily recital of the Divine Office.[58]

Compared to these early traditions of Latin Christian versifiers, which were mainly devoted to writing texts for a Christian community and within the boundaries of a well-established tradition, Petrarch's endeavor is more clearly aligned with asserting his own *auctoritas* as spiritual writer through a direct connection and creative dialogue with the Psalmic authorial voice par excellence, the penitent sinner David, to whom, in *Fam.* 22.10 to Francesco Nelli, Petrarch refers as "meus poeta."[59] By engaging directly with David, Petrarch marks a major shift from the Psalms as the collective, liturgical "voice of the church" to a more personal, intimate, and introspective spiritual dimension. Rather than the voice of an entire people—Jewish or Christian—assembled in liturgical prayer, Petrarch's psalms' focus is inward, on the inner conflicts of the poet-penitent and self-proclaimed sinner and his unique personal redemptive journey, one that is still universal in scope, yet more personal and intimate. Put simply, with Petrarch's psalms we move from the Psalms as official prayer and liturgy of the people to the psalms as personal liturgy of the penitent self.

To acknowledge the devotional and liturgical sources of Petrarch's *devotiuncula* does not mean denying its equally unmistakable and more secular poetic roots. Petrarch's psalms, in fact, are notable for their generic hybridity and occupy a space somewhere in between the Petrarchan prayers, written specifically for liturgical and devotional use, the Latin poem in praise of Mary Magdalene, and the lyrical prayers that are an integral part of the personal, spiritual, and redemptive journey of the self in *Rvf.*, and these were in turn, and not surprisingly, influenced by the Psalms themselves.[60]

The typical elegiac elements of tearful lament, loss, and grief, so predominant in *Rvf.*, mirror and echo the penitential-purgatorial tone, centered on the lexicon of *miseria*, at the core of both the traditional Psalms and Petrarch's own.

The elegiac and penitential qualities of Petrarch's intimate and personal psalmody, however, are no less effective in allowing readers to recognize themselves in the penitent self at the center. Indeed, Petrarch's introspective, confessional verses were consistent and in harmony with the late medieval development of private forms of devotion.[61] Already in Petrarch's time, his psalms could have circulated among close friends, even before and after Sagremor's own request to have a copy;[62] they were read and recited not only in religious and monastic communities, including that of the Carthusians, but also in other more secular devotional contexts.[63]

David the psalmist was not Petrarch's only source and authorial model in writing his *devotiuncula*. As with his other writings, Petrarch's self-fashioning in terms of and, at times, against his predecessors—religious and nonreligious, classical or Christian—is a well-known and documented strategy evident throughout the Petrarchan corpus. In the specific case of his psalms, he engaged directly with some of the "usual suspects" who emerge often explicitly—Augustine—or more obliquely—Dante.

The bishop of Hippo is not only relevant for our discourse as the one who, after Cassiodorus (490–585), may have been instrumental in the genesis of the series of the traditional seven penitential Psalms. His *Enarrationes in Psalmos* had a profound impact on Petrarch's own study of scripture and the Psalms as well as his own attempt at writing psalmic verses.[64] Moreover, it is in the Paris, MS Latin 1944, containing Augustine's *Enarrationes* on the last fifty psalms, that Petrarch will add a pro-memoria on March 21, 1337. The *Considerare debemus* has been rightfully considered a programmatic statement for the seven psalms as its structure presents a premise followed by six "outcomes" centered on the notion of prayer as the simple and confident expression of one's deepest desires, fears, and hopes.[65]

Moreover, well known to Petrarch, a devoted reader of the *Confessions*, was Augustine's arrival in Milan to seek out and find spiritual guidance from the city's saintly bishop Ambrose. Petrarch most likely knew well the episode in which the voices of the churchgoers singing Ambrose's hymns brought Augustine to true contrition and an overflowing of tears.[66] This episode may have inspired Petrarch to emulate Ambrose in writing verses that would enable the compunction of heart, the gift of tears of penance, and the confession of sins, all spiritual benefits usually ascribed, in patristic and monastic literature, to the reading and singing of Psalms and hymns.[67]

Less known, however, is the fact that Augustine had authored one of the first psalmic adaptations. His *Psalmus contra partem Donati* (393), in fact, is considered one of the earliest extant compositions in rhythmic Latin verse. Written against the Donatists, it presumably imitated the same verses sung in church by the Donatists, who had previously written similar doctrinal pamphlets in psalmic verses. Augustine's psalm was later included in the *Milleloquia Veritatis Sancti Augustini* (1345), a comprehensive Augustinian lexicon very popular in Petrarch's day. On the request of the author-compiler, Bartolomeo da Urbino, Petrarch even wrote some introductory verses praising the accomplishment of his friend.[68]

More importantly, the autobiographical model of Augustine's *Confessions* was central to Petrarch's placing the writing of his own conflicted self, front and center, in his psalms. Indeed, Petrarch's psalms are the most genuinely Augustinian of his religious writings. In fact, in his other religious works—where Augustine's "inward turn" is always in plain sight, in particular, in the *Secretum*—Petrarch mainly writes about the self in dialogue with itself, tormented by doubts and anxieties and unable to change or reach true conversion. In his psalms instead, just like in Augustine's *Confessions*, Petrarch probes his interiority in the form of prayer, where God is the main interlocutor and the only one who can ultimately dissipate anxieties and reveal the author's true self.

Among the first who paraphrased scriptural texts in the vernacular, Francis of Assisi and Dante were certainly known to Petrarch. In the *Commedia*, Dante had already fashioned his status as *scriba Dei* on that of the poet-penitent David. Thus Petrarch had to deal with the historical-literary circumstance of his predecessor's direct involvement with the Psalms and the figure of David before he could "occupy" the role of psalmist himself. The Davidic dimension of the first word uttered by the protagonist in the *Commedia*, "*Miserere* di me" (*Inf.* 1.65), registered in the commentary tradition, resonates in Petrarch's incipitarian "Heu michi misero" of his first psalm. In the *Purgatorio*—the cantica centered on penitence and the liturgical expression of it—Dante introduces his version of the Our Father (the *oratio super*

Pater Noster, in *Purg.* 11.1–21) as sung by those furthest from Christian humility, that is, the proud penitents who, stooped under heavy weights on their shoulders, are still pressed to face the "humble psalmist" (*Purg.* 10.65) carved into the side of the mountain on the first terrace of Purgatory as an emblem of humility. Indeed, throughout the *Purgatorio*, Dante will use verses from the traditional penitential Psalms and mainly from Psalm 50 (51), the *Miserere*, which reveal an arrangement centered on the themes of penitence and praise just like Petrarch's seven psalms.[69] Finally, in *Paradiso* 20.38, David, presented as the psalmist or "cantor de lo Spirito Santo" (the one who sang the praises of the Holy Spirit), becomes the model, with his Psalms, for Dante's *poema sacro*, as the *Commedia* is also a *teodia*, that is, a song, or hymn, praising God (*Par.* 25.70–75).[70]

With the *Canticle*, Francis revealed his deep knowledge and assimilation of scripture as well as his mnemonic and poetic ability to recompose, in order to praise God for his creation, biblical sources, which mainly include Psalm 148 and Daniel 3.52–90. Intended as a pastoral tool, Francis made clear, on his deathbed, that with his *Canticle* he expected to bring to the illiterate a scriptural text of praise that was usually sung in Latin by monks and friars as part of the office (at Sunday morning Lauds), but that remained mostly inaccessible to the illiterate masses.[71] Petrarch's strategic and unexpected insertion in his own sequence of a psalm of praise of the beauty of creation and the usefulness of God's gifts to mankind may well be modeled on Francis's, as we will see later on.[72]

Another important connection between Petrarch's psalms and the Poverello can be seen in the latter's significant influence on the official liturgical prayer of the church. It was in fact the liturgical needs of the mendicant orders, focused on bringing Christ directly out of cloistered monastic walls, that led to the widespread circulation and adoption of the simpler and more manageable "curial" breviary—bulky and expensive liturgical books were incompatible with the itinerant friars' preaching about Christ poor and crucified—which was the result of Innocent III's reform of the Divine Office, later imposed on all the churches of Rome by the Franciscan pope Nicholas III (r. 1277–80).[73] The same breviaries that we know Petrarch owned and used regularly, as noted earlier, are in fact the same "Roman" breviaries, as they were called, since they reproduced the Divine Office adopted by the papal court and then by the Franciscans.

xxxii   Introduction

The simplification and abridgement of the Divine Office was an important step in the development of "minor" offices centered on specific devotional practices and moments in the life of Christ, the Virgin, and the saints. The Poverello himself had authored a lengthy and elaborate cycle of prayers in Latin, the *Office of the Passion*, which can be seen as a likely precedent for Petrarch's own psalms.[74] Francis's *Office* mainly consists of fifteen psalms that he composed by drawing on specific verses of the scriptural Psalms, other scriptural books, and liturgical texts, in the typical monastic, mnemonic style of *lectio divina* where the words are pondered and ruminated until they become one's own and are indelibly impressed upon one's heart.[75]

Worth noting in this regard is also the fact that for Petrarch, Francis was an important model of ascetic, solitary life, as he writes in the second book of *Dvs*. In effect, it is Francis who, according to Petrarch, best exemplifies the three types of solitude he describes in the treatise: solitude of place, living far from the crowds and preferring the countryside; solitude of time, as Francis is said to have preferred the night hours; and solitude of the soul, since the Poverello was able to keep an intimate detachment even while being "pushed around by the crowds."[76] Moreover, of the three, spending the night in prayer was usually associated with the monastic practice of singing Psalms, a practice Petrarch was familiar with, as he reminds his brother, Gherardo: "In the middle of the night . . . refers to psalm singing at matins, since especially at that hour they are heard in your churches."[77]

PETRARCH'S PSALMS

Scholars agree that Petrarch's psalms were primarily inspired by the seven penitential Psalms of the liturgy: 6 (7), 31 (32), 37 (38), 50 (51), 101 (102), 129 (130), and 142 (143).[78] As poems of the remorseful soul crying out over one's failures and sins, these were usually recited during Lent, in rites of penance, and in association with the traditional and popular offices of the sick, the dying, and the dead.[79] First assembled from the entire book of Psalms by Cassiodorus, they have been rightly seen as a microcosm of the 150 scriptural Psalms.[80] The very origin of the Divine Office can be traced to the idea of reciting the psalms seven times a day, a tradition that Petrarch knew well. As noted earlier, in his letter to Gherardo, Petrarch cites the passage from Psalm 118.164 (119.164) in which the psalmist mentions the sevenfold moments of praise during the day and night: "So much was I pleased by the words of the Psalmist: 'Seven times I have praised you during the day' that since I took up this habit no activity has distracted me from it, not even once."[81] Petrarch's newly acquired habit involved rising at night for the nocturnal office, that is, matins, considered the most elaborate office. In his first eclogue, Petrarch had also clearly stressed the liturgical dimension of singing David's Psalms because at night "you will see a shepherd tuning notes of unrivalled sweetness" (vv. 55–56).[82]

The close relationship between Petrarch's seven psalms and the liturgical recitation or singing of the Psalms seven times a day is further confirmed by the closing doxology, "*Gloria Patri . . . et in secula seculorum. Amen,*" at the end of each of Petrarch's seven psalms. The *Gloria* was originally added at the end of the scriptural Psalms to mark the transition from their Jewish original setting to the early forms of Christian worship. According to Cassian (ca. 360–435), the use of the trinitarian doxology dates from the end of the fourth century in the monastic communities of France and was later used in Rome (fifth century).[83] In his *Rule*, St. Benedict mentions the recitation of the *Gloria* as a "common antiphon" to the psalms in the daily reciting of the Divine Office. It soon became universal throughout the Christian Church.[84]

Given this rich and multilayered liturgical context characterized by penitence and praise, it comes as no surprise that the main theme and tone in Petrarch's seven psalms revolve around the rich semantic range of the word *miseria*. Written in the time of his "misery," as Petrarch writes to Sagremor, the very incipit of the first Psalm reads, "Heu michi misero," echoing the incipitarian "Miserere mei" of the penitential Davidic Psalm 50 (51), which, in turn, implicitly alludes to the theme of lust. One of the seven deadly sins, lust is arguably the main reason for Petrarch to keep his own *Memoriale* where most of the entries start with "Heu" as well.[85]

Moreover, if we compare the internal arrangement of the traditional seven penitential Psalms with Petrarch's version, we find that Petrarch shows an intimate, almost certainly mnemonic, familiarity with the traditional penitential Psalms while also significantly reworking the main themes present in the originals. In the traditional sequence, Psalm 50 (51), the *Miserere*, is the central and fourth Psalm and is characterized by the theme of penitence and repentance. Moreover, it is preceded by three Psalms—6, 31 (32),

37 (38)—beseeching divine mercy and is followed by three Psalms—101 (102), 129 (130), 142 (143)—in which the formula "exaudi orationem meam" (hear my prayer) immediately points to the psalmist-petitioner imploring that his prayer be heard.[86]

In Petrarch's version, his first psalm echoes the traditional Psalm 6 (7) as it reproposes the figure of the penitent sinner oppressed by guilt and shame while invoking divine mercy. Similar to the Davidic Psalm 31 (32), Petrarch's second psalm highlights instead the joy and certainty of the sinner who feels God's forgiveness, though without neglecting the need for contrition. The certainty and exultance of Petrarch's second psalm is replaced in the third psalm by the voice of the penitent who invokes God's help to free him from the sins in which he has fallen and grant him eternal salvation and the will to save himself. There are clear references here to Psalm 37 (38), especially the first part, but typically Petrarchan is the lament over wasted time, the moral impasse, and the need of divine intervention to obtain an unwavering heart.

The second group of Petrarch's psalms, after the central psalm 4, which I examine more closely in the following pages, also resounds with the poet's intimate take on the penitential tone and themes of the traditional Psalms. Psalm 5 offers a personal rendition of several verses from the fifth traditional penitential Psalm 102 (103), especially the images of nocturnal torments, dissipated days, enemies, and inner conflicts. The assault of internal and external enemies becomes the central theme of psalm 6, where the penitent voice is in the end left almost lifeless and capable only of invoking divine help. The last psalm of the Petrarchan sequence takes us back to the image of overconfidence and self-conceit that ultimately leaves the penitent "I" of the poem in his habitual state of indecision, irresoluteness, and, ultimately, need of divine intervention.[87]

A clear and surprising departure from the overall penitential and redemptive dimension of the traditional sequence is evident instead in Petrarch's psalm 4. This central psalm, strikingly original and innovative, resonates with joyful imagery that evokes Francis's *Canticle of the Creatures*, as it resembles less a psalm of penitence and more a hymn of praise for creation and for all God's gifts to humanity: sky, sun, moon, stars, air, water, our body and soul.[88] We could almost discern in Petrarch's original substitution of Psalm 50 (51)—the quintessential penitential psalm, at the center of the traditional sequence—with a hymn of praise and thanksgiving the deliberate attempt to challenge, redefine, and replace the traditional Christian understanding of repentance with a classical humanist vision of salvation centered on the beauty and goodness of creation and a dignified conception of man as *imago Dei*.[89]

Further, psalm 4 clearly acts as a watershed between the first and second group of three psalms in Petrarch's sequence. On the one hand, it is preceded by three poems in which the focus is on the confession of sins and invocation for divine mercy. Here there is also a clear focus on the intimate and personal dialogue between the penitent self and God, where the poet-penitent not only recognizes his own faults but also mainly blames his own weakness for having fallen into sin. On the other hand, in the following three, more pronounced is the presence of external "enemies" or "external persecutors" whom the poet-penitent indicates as those who have contributed to or benefited from his fall. No longer an intimate, confessional dialogue, the exchange between the poet and God in this second group entails the presence of others who are mainly the ones to blame for the poet's downfall. It is only in the final psalm in Petrarch's sequence that the poet's own self is yet again recognized as the main and only enemy standing in the way of God's will.

More importantly, we can discern in Petrarch's overall rendering of the traditional Psalms another central aspect that runs through the entire sequence. There emerges, in fact, a gradual spiritual shift from a deeply felt sense of guilt to an unwavering hope in God's forgiveness signaled by the strategic use of the lexicon of "miseria," consistently present in all seven psalms, with its semantic interplay between terms referring to the sinner's misery (*miser/misero*) and those denoting God's mercy (*miseror/miseratio/misericordia*), for a total of twenty-one occurrences.[90]

Following this path, from the darkness of misery to the light of mercy, the focus on "miseria" emerges consistently in the first three psalms, while God's "misericordia," introduced more unequivocally into the central psalm 4, appears more conspicuously in the final three. As noted, psalm 1 begins with the expression, "Heu michi misero" (Oh, wretched me); "miseriarum" (miseries) appears in verse 11; and the psalm, the longest of the seven, ends with the imperative "miserere" (have mercy). After mentioning "miseratio Domini" (the Lord's mercy; v. 7), psalm 2 presents in adjacent verses "miseriarum mearum" (my miseries; v. 13) and "miserationum tuarum" (your acts of mercy; 14). This is the only psalm, in the first group of three, where "miseria" and its derivatives convey the meanings of both misery and mercy. It also ends, like psalm 1, with the invocation "miserere." Psalm 3 opens with the supplication "miserere" soon followed by the depiction of the poet-psalmist as "miser" (vv. 1 and 2); the poem ends with the invocation "miserere" and "miserias meas." Psalm 4, as noted, marks the gradual shift from "miser" and "miserere" to "misericordia" as it increasingly reveals the poet-penitent relying on God's infinite mercy: "misereberis" (you will have mercy; v. 2), "miseratus" (you had compassion) and "misericordia" (v. 20), ending with "miserere" before the doxology. Psalm 5 confirms this transitional movement from wretchedness ("miser") to "misericordia tua," closing with the final invocation "miserere." In psalm 6, the poet-psalmist expresses hope in God's mercy "misereberis" (v. 12), while psalm 7 closes with the poet-petitioner, once again, recognizing his being oppressed by indescribable "miseriis" (v. 20) but expressing hope in Christ who will sustain him "misericorditer" (with mercy; v. 22).

These lexical and semantic choices confirm a movement from penitence to praise to hope in God's mercy and forgiveness. It also reveals the gospel teaching underpinning Petrarch's psalms, that is, humility, the Davidic and monastic virtue par excellence, as a necessary condition for God's redemptive grace: only by acknowledging our weakness and proclivity to evil (as seen in the first three psalms) can we experience a sense of humbling and wonder facing God's greatness and goodness toward us (psalm 4) and hope in God's infinite mercy (final three psalms).

The confessional and redemptive dimension of Petrarch's psalms confirms his assimilation of another fundamental monastic teaching: nourished by the teachings of the prophets and apostles, the Christian penitent sings the psalms, as Cassian put it, "not as though they had been composed by the prophet," but as "if he himself had written them, as if this were his own private prayer uttered amid the deepest compunction of heart." Cassian goes on to state:

> Certainly he thinks of them as having been specially composed for him and recognizes that what they express was made real not simply once upon a time in the person of the prophet but that now, every day, they are being fulfilled in himself. . . . We see very clearly, as in a mirror, what is being said to us and we have a deeper understanding of it. Instructed

by our own experiences we are not really learning through hearsay but have a feeling for these sentiments as things that we have already seen.[91]

On a formal level, and as noted briefly earlier, Petrarch's psalms seem to reproduce the somewhat prose-like verses of Jerome's Latin translation of the Psalms as the most befitting for the tone of his compositions.[92] In *Fam.* 10.4.31, in fact, Petrarch clearly states that what characterizes David's voice is its hoarseness, the unceasing tears, suggesting that the poetic language of the Psalms is "rough" and "mournful." The emphasis on tears is important as it epitomizes in Petrarch's poetics the main traits of the Davidic style: lament and praise. This is particularly evinced in *Parthenias*, where, in contrast to the heroic poetry of Silvius-Petrarch's champions, Homer and Virgil, Monicus, a stand-in for Petrarch's Carthusian brother, Gherardo, proposes David who "tearful he is, pouring forth from his breast unmusical groanings" (v. 74).[93] In the following lines, however, Monicus stresses that David sings of God and the beauty of creation as well. He thus objects to Silvius's characterization of David's singing as "hoarse" (*raucum*), describing his voice instead as "firm" (*solida*) and "deep reaching into souls with mysterious sweetness" (vv. 103–4).[94] The poetic style of the Davidic Psalms is thus characterized, on the one hand, by the "hoarse" laments of the remorseful sinner and, on the other, by the "sweet" language of praise. As Giovanni Pozzi has observed, Petrarch's remarkable synthesis of biblical language reflects the overall centrality of the gift of tears in medieval spirituality: the sinner's tears of compunction and remorse ultimately lead to tears of joy and praise.[95] Pozzi also convincingly observes how this defense of the Davidic psalmody is well suited to Monicus, who embodies monastic life where the tears of the penitent soul are transformed into tears of love for God.

Monicus, thus, represents a religious, contemplative path to salvation through a withdrawal from the *negotium* of the world to a place where theology is the main focus, in contrast to Silvius's aspiration to scholarly fame through an engagement with the secular world and focus on poetry and the *studia humanitatis*. This contrast, however, is also between two different religious vocations: if Monicus represents the more austere call to monastic life, Silvius instead stands for the life of the *clericus*. This is suggested by the name "Monicus," which in *Fam.* 10.4.20 Petrarch writes "is appropriate since one of the Cyclops is named Monicus, as if he were one-eyed. Such a name seemed in a certain respect fitting for you since of the two eyes that we mortals usually use, one to gaze upon heavenly things and the other upon earthly ones, you renounced the one that beholds earthly things, being content with the better eye."[96]

Moreover, Petrarch's prose made to fit in the system of the *versi*, or poetic lines, reveals a deliberate intent to preserve the only poetic element kept by Jerome in his rendering of the Psalms.[97] His use of the *cursus*, in particular, of the dynamic *velox*, stressing throughout an intense movement of the penitent toward God's forgiveness and power, and the *tardus*, echoing instead a more static sluggishness and *acedia*, reveal the most fundamental aspects of Petrarch's poetics, one of inner conflict and oscillations of the soul caught between desire, sin, sloth, repentance, and praise.[98] The prosodic structure reproducing the Davidic Psalms and the fragmented style of penitential prayer reveal a movement deliberately closer to the meanders of a restless soul, one that stresses the harshness and asperity of the redemptive process and the misery of the human condition prone to sin. They echo the penitent's torments and cry for being at fault and tormented by sinful desires, most likely lust, as we have seen. It is after all the asperity of the sinner's tears that are necessary to deserve God's forgiveness, as Petrarch tells Sagremor at the end of *Sen.* 10.1.132: "through holy sighs and pious tears—which are the most efficacious way to break the hardness of sin and to quell and avert the wrath of God and receive His grace."[99]

By adopting and adapting the penitential and confessional dimension of guilt, misery, and penance of the traditional seven penitential Psalms to a more humanist idiom, expressing the universal condition of sinfulness and misery transformed in hope and trust in God's goodness and forgiveness, Petrarch ultimately confirms his understanding and mastery of a religious poetic style while providing a uniquely personal—but still universal—dimension to that ongoing and never-ending dialogue between humankind and the Invisible One.

Petrarch's Prayers

In the Petrarchan corpus, Petrarch's prayers no doubt remain among his least known and studied writings.[100] As a cleric who dedicated regular time to the recitation of the Divine Office, Petrarch must have found it easy to write, rewrite, and assemble prayers for his personal use. As a genre, prayers are often the result of the combination and fusion of traditional Christian religious and liturgical texts. Therefore, it should not surprise us that Petrarch's prayers often stem from the combination and the weaving together of pre-existent liturgical and scriptural texts with his own original additions, or with other patristic sources (especially Augustine).

The prayers that Petrarch penned over the course of his life, even on the margins of codices he owned, have never been assembled in a systematic corpus. In the manuscript tradition they often appear alongside his psalms but in a scattered and unsystematic manner. At times they are grouped under titles such as *Orationes contra tempestates aereas* and *Orationes quotidianae*, but these categorizations are inconsistent at best. Moreover, even though some are traditionally attributed to Petrarch, the authorship remains somewhat dubious. The prayers in the present edition are the ones selected and included in the edition for the centenary based on their unquestioned authorship. The first three are Petrarch's autographs and are written on the first two folios of the Parisian codex Bibliothèque Nationale, Lat. 2201. The next six fall into the *Orationes contra tempestates aereas* category. The final one was written for the night office, known as matins or vigil, a canonical hour of which Petrarch became particularly fond as attested by several of his writings.[101]

Petrarch's prayers are not only closely associated with his psalms for appearing often together in the manuscript tradition, but they also reveal a similar recourse to scriptural and liturgical sources, allusions to theological themes, and use of poetic and affective language. The Parisian codex, in which the three autographs appear (it also includes Petrarch's well-known list of *liber peculiares*), contains both Cassiodorus's *De anima* and Augustine's *De vera religione*. The latter most likely was the source of inspiration for Petrarch's first two prayers, written in prose, as they echo doctrinal beliefs present in Augustine's work. Most notably, Petrarch follows the bishop of Hippo in envisioning, at the very beginning of the first longest prayer, dated June 1, 1335, the union of soul and body with Christ's incarnation as supreme model. The second prayer, dated July 10, 1338, and the most copied in the manuscript tradition as *Oratione quotidiana*, is an abridged version of the first; and the third, the shortest of the group, a prayer belonging to the *contra tempestates* group, betrays Petrarch's evident recourse to ancient liturgical texts woven together according to his poetic and literary sensibility, which in the end take on a new and personal meaning.

The attribution to Petrarch of the *contra tempestates* group of prayers seems beyond doubt considering Petrarch's frequent descriptions of his fear of the sea, shipwrecks, and sea storms. True, Petrarch often uses these tropes metaphorically and as a counterpoint to his constant search for a quiet "port," a safe harbor against the storms and shipwrecks of life. However, in many of his works he goes to great lengths to portray himself as a "peregrinus ubique," who, against all odds, is able to witness, or survive, real sea storms and shipwrecks. This is particularly true of the Neapolitan storm and tsunami witnessed in Naples in 1343. It is on this occasion in fact that he solemnly declared that he would never again travel by sea.[102]

Petrarch's willingness to create his own liturgical and devotional texts sheds a fascinating light on his rhetorical strategies and compositional methods as well as on his religious sensibility, personal devotion, and piety while also offering rare glimpses into his inner thoughts and deepest emotions. If at the end of *Parthenias* the contest between Homer and Virgil, on one side, and David, on the other, seems to end in a tie, Petrarch's psalms and prayers bring us back to *Fam.* 22.10, where David emerges as the ideal winner.[103] Imaginary poetic contests aside, these often-overlooked compositions are an essential tool for anyone who wants to understand the multifaceted Petrarchan universe more fully.

Notes

1. *Seniles* (hereafter *Sen.*)15.5.20: "legens semper et scribens et Deum laudans." Latin texts of the *Seniles* are from *Res seniles*, 4 vols., ed. Silvia Rizzo and Monica Berté (Florence: Le Lettere, 2017), 4:248. The English translation is from Petrarch, *Letters of Old Age. Rerum senilium libri*, 2 vols., trans. Aldo S. Bernardo, Saul Levin, and Reta A. Bernardo (Baltimore: Johns Hopkins University Press, 1992), 2:572.

2. *Sen.* 15.5.18; *Res seniles*, 4:248; *Letters of Old Age*, 2:572.

3. Even in his invectives, where he is often at his most vitriolic and rancorous, Petrarch finds ways to draw on scripture and the Psalms. In *Invectives against a Physician*, for instance, he writes, "Mirari autem desines, si cogitare ceperis ex persona Cristi, qui verus sapientie Deus et ipse sapientia Patris est, in Psalmo centesimo primo dictum esse: 'Factus sum sicut nycticorax in domicilio'" (But you will cease to be surprised if you start to reflect on Psalm 101. Speaking in the person of Christ, who is the true God of wisdom and also the wisdom of the Father, the Psalmist says: "I am like an owl that lives in its habitat"); and a few paragraphs later: "Libet enim gloriari, sed in Domino, cui semper tum pro multis, tum pro hoc nominatim gratias agam: quod me valde dissimilem tui fecit" (I like to boast, but in the Lord, whom I always thank for many things, and to whom I give special thanks for making me so unlike you). In Francesco Petrarca, *Francesco Petrarca, Invectives*, ed. and trans. David Marsh (Cambridge, MA: Harvard University Press, 2003), 164–65, 166–67.

4. Petrarch left his *magnus* breviary to the Cathedral of Padua, in the person of the priest, Giovanni da Bocheta, "ut post eius obitum remaneat in sacristia ecclesie ipsius Paduane ad obsequium perpetuum presbyterorum, ut ipse presbyter Iohannes et alii orent si eis placeat, Christum et beatam Virginem pro me" (on the condition that after his death it is to remain in the sacristy of the said Cathedral of Padua for the perpetual use of the priests. May the said priest Giovanni and the other priests, if they please, pray to Christ and the blessed Virgin on my behalf). Theodore E. Mommsen, trans. and ed., *Petrarch's Testament* (Ithaca, NY: Cornell University Press, 1957), 82–83.

5. As James Hankins aptly put it, "There are many political Petrarchs." James Hankins, "The Unpolitical Petrarch: Justifying the Life of Literary Retirement," in *Et Amicorum: Essays on Renaissance Humanism and Philosophy in Honour of Jill Kraye*, ed. Anthony Ossa-Richardson and Margaret Meserve (Leiden: Brill, 2018), 7. However, Petrarch's support of Cola di Rienzo's failed endeavor was perhaps the most consequential as it meant not only a major ideological shift but also a falling out with his patrons, the Colonna family, and his subsequent relocation from Avignon to Italy.

6. On Petrarch's *Coronation Oration*, see Ernest H. Wilkins, "Petrarch's Coronation Oration" *PMLA* 68.5 (1953): 1241–50; Dennis Looney, "The Beginnings of Humanistic Oratory: Petrarch's *Coronation Oration*," in *Petrarch, a Critical Guide to the Complete Works*, ed. Armando Maggi and Victoria Kirkham (Chicago: University of Chicago Press, 2009), 131–40; Gerhard Regn and Bernhard Huss, "Petrarch's Rome: The History of the *Africa* and the Renaissance Project," *MLN* 124.1 (2009): 86–102; and, more recently, David G. Lummus, *City of Poetry* (Cambridge: Cambridge University Press, 2020), 114–20.

7. On the Divine Office in the Middle Ages, see Jonathan Black, "The Divine Office and Private Devotion in the Latin West," in *The Liturgy of the Medieval Church*, ed. Thomas Heffernan and E. Ann Matter (Kalamazoo: Medieval Institute, Western Michigan University, 2001), 45–71; Joseph Dyer, "The Singing of Psalms in the Early-Medieval Office," *Speculum* 64.3 (1989): 535–78; Edward J. Quigley, *The Divine Office: A Study of the Roman Breviary* (Project Gutenberg open access); Rebecca A. Baltzer and Margot Fassler, eds., *The Divine Office in the Latin Middle Ages Methodology and Source Studies, Regional Developments, Hagiography: Written in Honor of Professor Ruth Steiner* (Oxford: Oxford University Press, 2000); Joanne M. Pierce, *Medieval Christian Liturgy*, https://doi.org/10.1093/acrefore/9780199340378.013.84. On the liturgical singing of the Psalms in Benedict's *Rule*, see Nathan D. Mitchell, "*Ordo Psallendi* in the *Rule*: Historical Perspectives," *American Benedictine Review* 20 (1969): 505–18.

8. On the early forms of worship, see Robert Taft's seminal work, *The Liturgy of the Hours in East and West* (Collegeville, MN: Liturgical Press, 1986). On Petrarch's clerical status, see Ernest H. Wilkins, "Petrarch's Ecclesiastical Career," *Speculum* 28.4 (1953): 754–75; Ronald Martinez, "Places and Times of the Liturgy from Dante to Petrarch," in *Petrarch and Dante*, ed. Zygmunt Barański and Theodore J. Cachey Jr. (Notre Dame, IN: University of Notre Dame Press, 2009), 320–70, at 324, 326; Demetrio S. Yocum, *Petrarch's Humanist Writing and Carthusian Monasticism: The Secret Language of the Self* (Turnhout: Brepols, 2013), 142–55.

9. For a detailed description of the breviary, see Martinez, "Places and Times," 325; and Giulio Goletti, "Il breviario del Petrarca," in *Petrarca nel tempo: Tradizione lettori e immagini delle opere. Catalogo della mostra, Arezzo, Sottochiesa di San Francesco, 22 novembre 2003–27 gennaio 2004*, ed. Michele Feo (Pontedera: Bandecchi & Vivaldi, 2003), 513–15. On the portable format of late medieval books of hours, see Paul Saenger, "Books of Hours and the Reading Habits of the Later Middle Ages," in *The Culture of Print: Power and the Uses of Print in Early Modern Europe*, ed. Roger Chartier and trans. Lydia G. Cochrane (Princeton, NJ: Princeton University Press, 2016), 141–73.

10. See, e.g., *Familiares* (hereafter *Fam.*) 7.3.11, where he writes to Ludwig van Kempen, "Surrexi demum hora solita—consuetudinem meam nosti—dumque quotidianis laudibus Deo dictis, ex more manum calamo applicuissem" (I finally got up at the regular hour (you know my custom) and after having recited my daily praises to God, I took up my pen as is my custom). See also *Fam.* 10.5.27–29. Latin texts of the *Familiares* are from *Le familiari*, 4 vols., ed. Vittorio Rossi (Florence: Sansoni, 1968), 2:105; the English translation is from Petrarch, *Letters on Familiar Matters: Rerum familiarum libri*, 3 vols., trans. Aldo S. Bernardo (Albany: State University of New York Press, 1975; repr. Baltimore: Johns Hopkins University Press, 1982–85), 1:342.

11. Suffice to say here that all the hours of the office start with the versicles "Deus, in adiutorium meum intende / Domine, ad adiuvandum me festina" from Ps. 69 (70), vv. 1–2. Cassian, whose *Conferences* first introduced to Western Christianity the Desert Fathers' sevenfold system of recitation of the hours, considered these verses the ideal prayer: "Hujus igitur versiculi oratio, in adversis ut eruamur, in prosperis ut servemur ne extollamur, incessabili jugitate fundenda est. Hujus, inquam, versiculi meditatio in tuo pectore indirupta volvatur" (Our prayer for rescue in bad times and for protection in good times should be founded on this verse. The thought of this verse should be turning unceasingly in your heart). The Latin text is from PL 49, 0836B. The English translation is from *John Cassian Conferences*, trans. Colm Luibheid (New York: Paulist Press, 1985), 135.

12. On the significant role of the Psalms in medieval culture, see, in particular, Nancy Van Deusen, ed., *The Place of the Psalms in Intellectual Culture of the Middle Ages* (Albany: State University of New York Press, 1999); on the history of the Divine Office, see Black, "The Divine Office," 45–71.

13. See Pietro Paolo Gerosa, *Umanesimo cristiano del Petrarca* (Turin: Bottega d'Erasmo, 1966), 337 n. 75.

14. *Fam.* 22.10.10–11: "Huius ego Psalterium et vigilanti semper in manibus semperque sub oculis, et dormienti simul ac morienti sub capite situm velim"; *Le familiari*, 4:128; *Letters on Familiar Matters*, 3:233.

15. *Sen.* 15.5.21: "sed exercitia mea sunt assidue, preterea Cristum orans bonum vite exitum et misericordiam . . . unde nil suavius in labiis meis sonat quam daviticum illud: 'Delicta iuventutis mee et ignorantias meas ne memineris.'" *Res seniles*, 4:248; *Letters of Old Age*, 2:572.

16. *Fam.* 10.3.56: "De Psalterio enim non dubito te Ieronimi consilium sequi, ut e manibus tuis nunquam excidat . . . vitam omnem inter contemplationem ac psalmodiam et orationem lectionemque partire"; *Le familiari*, 2:300; *Letters on Familiar Matters*, 2:67.

17. On the liturgy of the hours in *Dvs.*, see Yocum, *Petrarch's Humanist Writing*, 161–75.

18. Latin citations of *Dor.* are from *De otio religioso*, ed. Giulio Goletti (Florence: Le Lettere, 2006), 16. English translations are from *Petrarch on Religious Leisure*, ed. and trans. Susan S. Schearer (New York: Italica, 2002), 3–4.

19. "psalterium ipsum daviticum sepe percurrere sum coactus, e quibus fontibus haurire studui non unde disertior fierem, sed melior, si possem, neque unde evaderem disputator maior, sed peccator minor." *De otio religioso*, 256–58; *On Religious Leisure*, 147.

20. On *lectio divina* and *Dor.*, see Romana Brovia, "'Vacate et Videte' il modello della 'lectio divina' nel 'De otio religioso,'" *Petrarchesca* 1 (2013): 77–91; and Yocum, *Petrarch's Humanist Writing*, 266–67.

21. Latin citations and English translations of Petrarch's first eclogue, *Parthenias*, are from *Petrarch's Bucolicum Carmen*, ed. and trans. Thomas G. Bergin (New Haven, CT: Yale University Press, 1974), 12–13. Later in life, in *Fam.* 22.10.7, Petrarch will write to Francesco Nelli, "Iamque oratores mei fuerint Ambrosius Augustinus Ieronimus Gregorius, philosophus meus Paulus, meus poeta David, quem ut nosti multos ante annos prima egloga Bucolici carminis ita cum Homero Virgilioque composui, ut ibi quidem victoria anceps sit" (Now my orators shall be Ambrose, Augustine, Jerome, and Gregory, my philosopher shall be Paul, and my poet David, whom, as you know, many years ago in the first eclogue of my *Bucolicum carmen* I so compared to Homer and Virgil as to leave the victory undecided). *Le familiari*, 4:127; *Letters on Familiar Matters*, 3:233. As Guido Martellotti points out, the premise for writing the psalms is already present in that first eclogue since David's Psalms are here not only considered as testimony of faith, or religious travail, but also as poetry worthy to be compared to the verses of Homer and Virgil and worthy of poetic emulation. Michele Feo and and Silvia Rizzo, eds., *Guido Martellotti: Scritti petrarcheschi* (Padua: Antenore, 1983), 263–64.

22. *Fam.* 10.4.3: "Vox autem 'rauca' David et 'lacrimarum' assiduitas et repetitum sepe nomen 'Ierosolime' obicitur propter asperum prima facie et flebilem stilum et quia revera in Psalmis crebra illius urbis vel historica vel allegorica mentio est" (David's voice is said to be hoarse, and reference is made to his unceasing tears and his constant repetition of the name of Jerusalem to suggest that at first sight his style appears rough and mournful, and that his psalms frequently mention that city either historically or allegorically). *Le familiari*, 2:309; *Letters on Familiar Matters*, 2:75.

23. The poem in Latin exameters in praise of Mary Magdalene, dedicated to Philippe de Cabassoles, appears at the end of the letter he sent to Cabassoles, *Sen.* 15.15. See Ugo Dotti, *Vita di Petrarca* (Turin: Aragno, 2014), 65.

24. See E. Ann Matter, "Petrarch's Personal Psalms (*Psalmi penitentiales*)," in Maggi and Kirkham, *Petrarch, a Critical Guide*, 219–27; Martinez, "Places and Times." More recent valuable studies include Lorenzo Geri, "Varia fortuna del Petrarca 'monastico,'" in *Petrarca, l'Italia, l'Europa: Sulla varia fortuna di Petrarca, Bari, 20–22 maggio 2015*, ed. Davide Canfora (Bari: Edizioni di pagina, 2016), 171–82; Ester Pietrobon, "*Tam efficaciter utinam quam inculte:* Modelli liturgici e stile monastico nei *Psalmi penitentiales*," *Petrarchesca* 7 (2019): 47–65; and Mattia Boccuti, "L'umile salmista e il poeta laureato," *Italica* 98.2 (2021): 254–66. More recently, Erminia Ardissino's chapter "Salmi e preghiere di Petrarca" in her book *Poesia in forma di preghiera: Svelamenti dell'essere da Francesco d'Assisi ad Alda Merini* (Rome: Carocci, 2023), 137–53, deserves mention. I would like to express my gratitude to Ardissino for sharing her chapter, even though the current volume was already in the proofs stage when I received it. Among the Italian editions, Roberto Gigliucci, *Salmi penitenziali* (Rome: Salerno, 1997), offers a concise yet sophisticated introduction and commentary.

25. The strongest argument for dating Petrarch's psalms sometime between 1347 and 1348 is Guido Martellotti's: "Il contenuto dell'egloga [*Parthenias*] mi sembra escludere senza altro l'ipotesi . . . di una composizione dei *Salmi* anteriore al 1347, data di composizione di essa: ché l'invito di Monico non si capirebbe se il Petrarca si fosse già allora cimentato nella imitazione della poesia davidica, né si caprirebbero le obiezioni di Silvio che, almeno sul principio, trova quella poesia 'roca e lacrimosa'. . . . Certo mi sembra . . . che la composizione dei *Salmi* sia posteriore a quella della prima egloga (che è del 1347), probabile che la segua a breve distanza. Nulla vieta di supporla del 1348 come vuole Casali. Tale data si conviene a un'opera che si colloca idealmente sulla stessa linea del *De vita solitaria* (1346) e, soprattutto, del *De otio religioso* (1347)" (The content of the eclogue [*Parthenias*] seems to me to exclude the hypothesis . . . of a composition of the psalms prior to 1347, the date of composition of the eclogue, because Monicus's invitation would not be understood if Petrarch had already tried his hand with the imitation of Davidic poetry, nor would we be able to understand the objections of Silvio who, at least at the beginning, finds that poetry 'hoarse and tearful.' . . . It certainly seems to me . . . that the composition of the psalms is later than that of the first eclogue (which dates back to 1347), probably following it soon after. Nothing prevents us from assuming it dates back to 1348 as Casali suggests. This date is appropriate for a work that is ideally placed on the same line as *De vita solitaria* [1346] and, above all, *De otio religioso* [1347]). See Feo and Rizzo, *Guido Martellotti: Scritti petrarcheschi*, 263–64. Other possible evidence for dating it to 1348, which to my knowledge has never been advanced before, has to do with Petrarch's *Memoriale*, a personal diary of sorts appearing on the end pages of a manuscript, MS Paris Lat.

2923, which Petrarch owned. The manuscript, annotated by Petrarch, contains the correspondence between Abelard and Héloïse and also Berengar of Poitiers's invective against the Carthusians. Pierre de Nolhac published it (in *Pétrarque et l'humanisme* [Paris: Champion, 1907], vol. 2, excursus VI), and it supposedly records the dates in which Petrarch felt tempted by the flesh. It starts with the date April 21, 1344. The entries specify date and time of day. According to the entries, Petrarch felt tempted for the next year and a half, being free from lustful desires instead for the next two and a half years, that is, during the time he started to work on *Dvs.* and *Dor.* (1346–47). He struggled again with carnal desires in May 1348 until August 2, 1349, the last date recorded and probably the last time Petrarch fell into temptation. Also worthy of note is the fact that the elegiac tone of lament and grief rendered by the interjection "heu," appears almost at the beginning of each line, thus echoing not only the similar expression "Hei michi!" in *Parthenias* (v. 11), but, more importantly, the *incipit* of Petrarch's first psalm, "Heu michi misero," which in turn recalls David's own *Miserere mei* in Ps. 50 (51), thus underlying the sense of guilt and *miseria* in which Petrarch felt he had fallen and thus echoing David's own struggles with lust. On this topic, and in relation to Petrarch's claims of chastity since 1344, see Ronald Witt, "Petrarch, Creator of the Christian Humanist," in *Petrarch and Boccaccio*, ed. Igor Candido (Berlin: De Gruyter, 2018), 71–73. However, if the psalms were written between 1347 and 1348, it remains unclear why Petrarch would not mention them in his letter to Gherardo, *Fam.* 10.4 (Petrarch dates the letter December 2, and the general consensus is that it was written in 1349), in which he offers his most detailed discussion of the Psalms as theological poetry and where, in his explication of *Parthenias*, he reiterates his wish to bring to a happy conclusion his *Africa*. As far as I can determine, no one has yet asked this question about such an evident omission. On the dating question, see also Martinez, "Places and Times," 327 and n. 52; Marino Casali, "Per una più precisa datazione dei 'Salmi Penitenziali' del Petrarca," *Humanitas* 10 (1955): 696–704; Donatella Coppini, *Psalmi penitentiales; Orationes* (Florence: Le Lettere, 2010), 12.

26. Among the friends and patrons who died of the plague are Franceschino degli Albizzi, Cardinal Colonna, and King Robert of Naples, the dedicatee of the *Africa*.

27. Petrarch's higher esteem for the Carthusian order over other monastic orders is best stated in *Fam.* 10.4.28: "Limen intra quod Silvium Monicus invitat, Cartusiensium ordo est, quem nemo certe deceptus, ut multos ex aliis ordinibus, nemo intrat invitus" (The threshold that Monicus invites Silvius to cross is the Carthusian order, which no one enters by deception or against his will as in many other orders). *Le familiari*, 2:308; *Letters on Familiar Matters*, 2:74.

28. The *Bucolicum carmen*, which contains several "political" eclogues—including the fifth sent to Cola di Rienzo—was mostly planned and written between 1346 and 1347 as well.

29. The letter is *Dispersa* 73, written by Petrarch most likely on May 24, 1371, from Arquà. See Francesco Petrarca, *Lettere disperse*, ed. Alessandro Pancheri (Milan-Parma: Fondazione Pietro Bembo–U. Guanda, 1994), 474–89.

30. In *Fam.* 10.3. On the presence of monastic themes in Petrarch's works, see Giles Constable, "Petrarch and Monasticism," in *Francesco Petrarca Citizen of the World: Proceedings of the World Petrarch Congress Washington, D.C., April 6–13, 1974*, ed. Aldo S. Bernardo (Padua: Antenore, 1980), 53–99; Jean Leclercq, "Temi monastici nell'opera del Petrarca," *Lettere italiane* 43 (1991): 42–54. On Petrarch's "monastic" style, see Lorenzo Geri, "Varia fortuna del Petrarca 'monastico,'" 171–82; and Pietrobon, "*Tam efficaciter utinam quam inculte*," 47–65.

31. *Fam.* 10.3.26–27: "ille quidem evolavit, ego nullo iam laqueo tentus sed visco consuetudinis pessime delinitus, alas explicare nequeo et ubi vinctus fueram, solutus hereo." *Le familiari*, 2:292–93; *Letters on Familiar Matters*, 2:61.

32. See *Fam.* 4.1.9; *Le familiari*, 1:155; *Letters on Familiar Matters*, 1:174.

33. *Fam.* 10.3.26–27: "Quid cause est nisi quod 'contritis' pari conditione 'laqueis,' nequaquam quod sequitur par fuit, 'adiutorium nostrum in nomine Domini'? Cur autem hanc daviticam cantilenam tanto concentu ceptam tam dissona voce complevimus?" *Le familiari*, 2:292–93; *Letters on Familiar Matters*, 2:62. The fact that Psalm 123.8 (124.8) was used in the ordination ceremonies of clerics, as Martinez cogently observes, makes the divergence between the two brothers' religious paths all the more tangible. Martinez goes on to observe, "Petrarch constructed a chiasmus, persistently characterizing the religious, who are in fact bound by a rule, as free of bondage, but thinking of himself as bound." Martinez, "Places and Times," 326.

34. The words *Deus* and *Dominus*, used throughout the Psalter to address God, appear in each of the seven Petrarchan psalms, which along with the doxology confirm their nature as religious poems. See Matter, "Petrarch's Personal Psalms," 224.

35. The many surviving manuscripts and the early print editions of Petrarch's psalms testify to their wide circulation and popularity, particularly in connection with the works of the Carthusian monk Ludolph of Saxony (ca. 1300–1377), author of a famous and influential *Vita Iesu Christi* and *Expositio in Psalterium Davidis*. Donatella Coppini lists 138 manuscripts containing Petrarch's psalms. With Erwin Rauner's online cataloging tool (http://www.erwin-rauner.de/Schriftenverz.htm), which also includes Billanovich's count, the number of manuscripts jumps to 162. Lorenzo Geri's survey of surviving manuscripts for

copies of Petrarch's psalms reports the following: nonmonastic provenance (26); monastic provenance (10). The monastic copies come from mainly Benedictine (6) and Carthusian houses (2). I wish to thank Geri for sharing these findings. See also Geri, "Varia fortuna del Petrarca 'monastico,'" 182–83. Worth noting here is also the pivotal role that the Carthusian order played in transmitting Petrarch's writings in northern Europe, which were particularly influential in *devotio moderna* circles.

36. See in particular Biblioteca Medicea Laurenziana, Conv. Soppr. 381, where on the front leaf it says, "Isti sunt septem Psalmi Poenitentiales quondam a Francisco Petrarcha explanati ad devotionem omnium populorum: et qui cum magna devotione triginta diebus dixerit centum dies indulgentiae habet. Et post psalmos est oratio, quae si ab hominibus dicta fuerit quotidie, in mortem suam videbit virginem Mariam" (These are the *Seven Penitential Psalms* once set out by Francesco Petrarch for the devotion of all people. Whoever recites them with great devotion for thirty days will receive one hundred days of indulgence. After the psalms, there is a prayer, and if recited daily by individuals, they will behold the Virgin Mary at the hour of their death). In *Codici latini del Petrarca nelle biblioteche fiorentine*, ed. Michele Feo (Florence: Le Lettere, 1991), 320; Paolo Pintacuda, "Una traduzione spagnola dei *Salmi penitenziali* petrarcheschi: Studio ed edizione," in *Francesco Petrarca l'opera latina: Tradizione e fortuna*, ed. Luisa Secchi Tarugi (Florence: Franco Cesati Editore, 2004), 391–418.

37. *Sen.* 10.1.132: "Psalmos septem misi quos in miseriis dudum meis ipse michi composui tam efficaciter—utinam—quam inculte . . . leges eos qualescumque sunt, idque patientius facies si hos quidem ipsos et te petisse et me, multos ante annos, luce una nec integra dictasse, memineris." *Res seniles*, 3:140; *Letters of Old Age*, 2:357. On Petrarch's *inculte* style, see Vincenzo Fera, "Petrarca e la poetica dell'incultum," *Studi medievali e umanistici* 10 ([2012] 2015): 9–87, esp. 9–33; and Pietrobon, "*Tam efficaciter utinam quam inculte*," 61–65.

38. In his writings, Petrarch never referred to his psalms as "penitential." However, the designation is consistently present in the manuscript tradition and the *editio princeps* of 1473. Hence it has become the generally accepted title.

39. As Michael Graves notes, "It is clear from Epistle 106 that Jerome did not think he had produced a literal word-for-word translation in the Gallican Psalter and that he did not approve of corrections along these lines." In Michael Graves, *Jerome, Epistle 106 (on the Psalms)* (Atlanta, GA: SBL Press, 2022), 62. On Petrarch's breviary and familiarity with both the *Vetus Latina* and the *Vulgata* versions of the Bible, see Giulio Goletti, "*Scriptura qua utimur:* La Bibbia del Petrarca," *Quaderni petrarcheschi* 17–18 (2005–6): 629–77; Giovanni Pozzi, "Petrarca, i padri e soprattutto la Bibbia," *Studi petrarcheschi* 6 (1989): 125–69; and Edoardo Fumagalli, "Petrarca e la Bibbia," in *La Bibbia nella letteratura italiana:*

Dal Medioevo al Rinascimento, ed. Pietro Gibellini (Brescia: Morcelliana, 2009), 5:271–304. On Jerome's three versions of the Psalms, see Scott Goins, "Jerome Psalters," in *The Oxford Handbook of the Psalms*, ed. William P. Brown (Oxford: Oxford University Press, 2014), 185–98.

40. It is worth noting that Jerome does not delve into the topic of meter in his commentaries on the Old Testament. See Robert Graves, *Jerome's Hebrew Philology: A Study Based on His Commentary on Jeremiah* (Leiden: Brill, 2007), 23.

41. *Fam.* 10.4.1: "poeticam esse de Deo." *Le familiari*, 2:301; *Letters on Familiar Matters*, 2:70.

42. Dante held a different opinion, as he clearly stated in *Convivio* 1.7.14: "E però sappia ciascuno che nulla cosa per legame musaico armonizzata si può della sua loquela in altra transmutare sanza rompere tutta sua dolcezza ed armonia" (Therefore everyone should know that nothing harmonized according to the rules of poetry can be translated from its native tongue into another without destroying all its sweetness and harmony). Thus the Psalms "sono sanza dolcezza di musica e d'armonia" (lack the sweetness of music and harmony) and "tutta quella dolcezza venne meno" (all their sweetness was lost) in the "prima transmutazione" (first translation) from Hebrew into Greek. *Convivio* 1.7.15. Both Latin and English citations are from the Princeton Dante Project: https://dante.princeton.edu/. On the term "musaico," see Alessandro Niccoli, *Enciclopedia dantesca* (1970), https://www.treccani.it/enciclopedia/musaico_%28Enciclopedia-Dantesca%29/.

43. "sensibus intende, qui si veri salubresque sunt, quolibet stilo illos amplectere." *Fam.* 10.4, 8–9; *Le familiari*, 2:303; *Letters on Familiar Matters*, 2:70–71.

44. "dumosos colles silvasque pererro . . . Dulcius hic quanto media sub nocte videbis / Psallere pastorem! Reliquorum oblivia sensim / Ingeret ille tibi . . . Urget amor muse." *Petrarch's Bucolicum Carmen*, 2–15. I find convincing the argument, made recently by David Lummus, that the presence of Dante (in the figure of Monicus/Gherardo/Polyphemus) in *Parthenias* and *Fam.* 10.4, a presence described by Albert Ascoli as "hidden in plain sight," is not necessarily a challenge to Dante's claim to be *theologus-poeta* or *scriba dei* in order to assert a Latin, classical, humanistic poetics, as Ascoli has argued. In Lummus's reading, what Petrarch is actually enacting, through the reference to Polyphemus's cave entered by force (taken directly from Dante's second eclogue to Giovanni del Virgilio), is "the heroic takeover of the place of theological Davidic poetry that Dante and Monicus inhabit." The fact that Petrarch would compose his seven psalms almost certainly around the time of *Parthenias* and *Fam.* 10.4, a crucial detail often overlooked in discussions of both, would confirm this view. In other words, though covertly (but forcefully) staking out his opposition to Dante (while also being clearly indebted

4 Introduction

to him), Petrarch is appropriating for himself both the sacred and the secular, the Christian and the classical, the scriptural and the humanist, the Davidic and the Virgilian. See Lummus, *City of Poetry*, 135–36; and Albert R. Ascoli, "Blinding the Cyclops," in Barański and Cachey, *Petrarch and Dante*, 114–73. On the contrast between Silvius-Petrarch and Monicus-Gherardo, see also Thomas Greene, "Petrarch Viator: The Displacements of Heroism," in *The Vulnerable Text: Essays on Renaissance Literature* (New York: Columbia University Press, 1986), 18–45; and Giuseppe Mazzotta, "Humanism and Monastic Spirituality," in *The Worlds of Petrarch* (Durham, NC: Duke University Press, 1993), 147–66.

Worth noting also is Petrarch's recourse to the myth of Orpheus in *Parthenias*, which, in Zygmunt Barański's perceptive reading, conveys a nuanced view of the connection between theology and poetry as well as the poet's own unresolvable personal conflicts. See Zygmunt Barański, "'Io mi rivolgo indietro a ciascun passo' (Rvf 15. 1): Petrarch, the Fabula of Eurydice and Orpheus, and the Structure of the Canzoniere," in *Dante, Petrarch, Boccaccio: Literature, Doctrine, Reality* (Cambridge: Legenda, 2020), 393–416, at 403–8. See also Mazzotta, "Humanism," 154–59.

45. On questions related to the dating of Petrarch's psalms, see above n. 25.

46. See in particular Augustine's admission (*Confessions* 3.4) that it was Cicero's *Hortensius*, not scripture, that first led him to discover Christian truth; and also *De doctrina christiana* 2.25–28 where "pagan" learning is deemed useful. See also Jerome's well-known dream (in which an angel flogs him for being more of a "Ciceronian" than a Christian) in his famous letter to Eustochium (22).

47. On this topic, see Gerosa, *Umanesimo cristiano del Petrarca*, 293–316; Ronald Witt, *In the Footsteps of the Ancients: The Origins of Humanism from Lovato to Bruni* (Leiden: Brill, 2000); Witt, "Petrarch, Creator of the Christian Humanist," 71–73; Yocum, *Petrarch's Humanist Writing*, 256–65.

48. See Petrarch's letter to Boccaccio, *Sen.* 1.5, in which he presents an impressive range of arguments in favor of classical studies. For example, he observes that the church fathers would not have been able to do justice to Christianity or defend it against heresies without the knowledge and eloquence learned from the Latin classical authors.

49. See Lino Leonardi, Caterina Menichetti, and Sara Natale, eds., *Le traduzioni italiane della Bibbia nel Medioevo: Catalogo dei manoscritti (secoli XIII–XV)* (Florence: Edizioni del Galluzzo, 2018), xv–xxvii.

50. On the pseudo-Dantean vernacular *Sette salmi*, which are actually post-Petrarchan, see Ester Pietrobon, "Fare penitenza all'ombra di Dante: Questioni di poesia e devozione nei *Sette salmi*," *L'Alighieri* 51 (2018): 63–80. On the influ-

ence of Petrarch's psalms on Renaissance authors such as Bernardo Tasso and Bartolomeo Arnigio, see Ester Pietrobon, *La penna interprete della cetra: I "Salmi" in volgare e la poesia spirituale italiana nel Rinascimento* (Rome: Edizioni di Storia e Letteratura, 2019); and Lorenzo Geri and Ester Pietrobon, eds., *Lirica e sacro tra Medioevo e Rinascimento: (secoli XIII–XVI)* (Canterano [RM]: Aracne Editrice, 2020). Worth noting here is that Petrarch's psalms, along with the *Rvf.*, had a major impact on the early modern English tradition of versifying in psalmic style. On this topic, see Deirdre Serjeantson, "The Book of Psalms and the Early Modern Sonnet," *Renaissance Studies* 29.4 (2015): 632–49. In 1612, George Chapman, best known as a playwright and translator of Homer, translated, or better yet, freely adapted, Petrarch's psalms into English under the title *Seven Penitentiall Psalmes*. See Alec Ryrie and Jessica Martin, eds., *Private and Domestic Devotion in Early Modern Britain* (Farnham: Ashgate, 2012), 229–31.

51. Saenger, "Books of Hours," 142.

52. On this topic, see Jacques Fontaine, *Naissance de la poésie dans l'occident chrétien: Esquisse d'une histoire de la poésie latine chrétienne du IIIe au VIe siècle. Avec une préface de Jacques Perret* (Paris: Études Augustiniennes, 1981); Charles Witke, *Numen Litterarum: The Old and the New in Latin Poetry from Constantine to Gregory the Great* (Leiden: Brill, 1971); Carl P. E. Springer, *The Gospel as Epic in Late Antiquity: The Paschale Carmen of Sedulius* (Leiden: Brill, 1988); Michael Roberts, *Biblical Epic and Rhetorical Paraphrase in Late Antiquity* (Liverpool: Francis Cairns, 1985).

53. "quorum soluta oratione nichil omnino, metrica vero passim cernuntur opuscula." *Fam.* 10.4.8. *Le familiari*, 2:303; *Letters on Familiar Matters*, 2:70.

54. "pinguem . . . campum . . . laurea nusquam . . . viridis non gloria serti . . . fragilis vox." *Bucolicum carmen*, tenth eclogue, vv. 313–18. In *Petrarch's Bucolicum Carmen*, 172–75.

55. See Gigliucci, *Salmi penitenziali*, 12; Matter, "Petrarch's Personal Psalms," 224; and Marco Ariani, *Petrarca* (Rome: Salerno, 1999), 130.

56. Joseph Szövérffy, *A Concise History of Medieval Latin Hymnody* (Leyden: Classical Folia Editions, 1985), 1–7.

57. See Emma Hornby, "Pia dictamina," in *The Canterbury Dictionary of Hymnology* (Canterbury Press), https://hymnology.hymnsam.co.uk/.

58. See Yocum, *Petrarch's Humanist Writing*, 155–75.

59. *Fam.* 22.10.7; *Le familiari*, 4:127; *Letters on Familiar Matters*, 3:233.

60. See Nicolò Maldina, "Penitenza ed elegia nel *Canzoniere* del Petrarca," in *La Bibbia in poesia*, ed. Rosanna Pettinelli et al. (Rome: Bulzoni, 2015), 17–33. On the notable similarities between the book of Psalms, as a collection of poems attributed to David, and Petrarch's choices in shaping his own collection of ver-

nacular poems, see Nicolò Maldina, "Petrarca e il libro dei 'Salmi': Materiali per la struttura dei 'Rerum Vulgarium Fragmenta,'" *Lettere italiane* 66.4 (2014): 543–58.

61. For a history of reading and writing in the Middle Ages, see especially the work of Paul Saenger: *Space between Words: The Origins of Silent Reading* (Stanford: Stanford University Press, 1997); and "Silent Reading: Its Impact on Late Medieval Script and Society," *Viator* 13 (1982): 367–414.

62. See *Sen.* 10.1.132; *Res seniles*, 3:140; *Letters of Old Age*, 2:357.

63. See Geri, "Varia fortuna del Petrarca 'monastico,'" 182.

64. On Augustine and the traditional seven Psalms, see Michael S. Driscoll, "The Seven Penitential Psalms: Their Designation and Usages from the Middle Ages Onwards," *Ecclesia Orans* 17 (2000): 153–201; Clare Costley King'oo, *Miserere Mei* (Notre Dame, IN: University of Notre Dame Press, 2012), 1–24. On the influence of the *Enarrationes in Psalmos* on Petrarch's own *Psalmi*, see Donatella Coppini, "Petrarca, i salmi e il codice parigino latino 1994 delle 'Enarrationes' di Agostino," in *Petrarca e Agostino*, ed. Roberto Cardini and Donatella Coppini (Rome: Bulzoni, 2004), 19–38.

65. See Pietrobon, "*Tam efficaciter utinam quam inculte*," 53.

66. See Augustine, *Confessions*, 9.6.14.

67. The two terms, "psalm" and "hymn," according to Isidore of Seville (ca. 560–636), were synonyms. See *Etymologiae* 6.2.15: "Psalmorum liber Graece psalterium, Hebraice nabla, Latine organum dicitur. Vocatus autem Psalmorum [liber] quod, uno propheta canente ad psalterium, chorus consonando respondent. Titulus autem in psalmis Hebraicus ita est, Sepher Thehilim, quod interpretatur volumen hymnorum" (The book of Psalms is called in Greek the Psalter [Psalterium], in Hebrew Nabla, and in Latin Organum. It is called the book of Psalms because one prophet would sing to a psaltery-lute and the chorus would respond in the same tone. Moreover, the Hebrew title heading the psalms is this: Sepher Thehilim, which means scroll of hymns). The Latin text is from Wallace Martin Lindsay, *Isidori Hispalensis Episcopi: Etymologiarvm sive originvm*. Vol. 1, *Libros I–X* (Oxford: Oxford University Press, 2016), 219–20. The English translation is from Stephen A. Barney, *The Etymologies of Isidore of Seville* (Cambridge: Cambridge University Press, 2006), 136.

68. See Elena Giannarelli, "Quale e quanto Agostino ai tempi del Petrarca," in Cardini and Coppini, *Petrarca e Agostino*, 1–17; 15; Ugo Mariani, *Il Petrarca e gli Agostiniani* (Rome: Edizoni di Storia e Letteratura, 1946), 49–53.

69. See Martinez, "Places and Times," 327–28.

70. In *Fam.* 10.4.6–7, Petrarch refers to Christ's life as "sacrum . . . poema." As Martinez points out, this could be seen as a reference to the liturgy and the Psalter but also to Dante's "poema sacro." See Martinez, "Places and Times," 337.

The Italian text and English translation are from Robert Hollander, *Paradiso* (New York: Doubleday, 2007).

71. "He composed a melody for these words and taught it to his companions so they could repeat it. . . . He said that he wanted one of them who knew how to preach, first to preach to the people. After the sermon, they were to sing the Praise of the Lord as minstrels of the Lord." The English translation is from Regis J. Armstrong et al., eds., *Francis of Assisi: Early Documents*, vol. 2 (Hyde Park, NY: New City Press, 1999), 186.

72. Among the subsequent vernacular expressions of religious piety worth mentioning here is the Italian lauda, which played another crucial role in shaping Petrarch's spiritual consciousness and devout writing.

73. See S. J. P. Van Dijk, *Origins of the Modern Roman Liturgy: The Liturgy of the Papal Court and the Franciscan Order in the Thirteenth Century* (Westminster: Newman Press, 1960); J. D. Crichton, "The Office in the West: The Early Middle-Ages," in *The Study of Liturgy*, ed. C. James, G. Wainwright, and E. Yarnald (Oxford: Oxford University Press), 1978; and Dominic F. Scotto, TOR, "St. Francis and the Spirit of the Liturgy," *The Cord* 32.1 (1982): 16.

74. On Francis and Franciscans as influences on Petrarch, see Anna Maria Voci, *Petrarca e la vita religiosa: Il mito umanista della vita eremitica* (Rome: Istituto storico italiano per l'età moderna e contemporanea, 1983), 67–81; Timothy Kircher, *The Poet's Wisdom: The Humanists, the Church, and the Formation of Philosophy in the Early Renaissance* (Leiden: Brill, 2005), 22–24; and Rodney J. Lokaj's two articles: "Petrarca-alter Franciscus, ovvero un'ascesa francescana del Monte Ventoso," *Il Veltro. Rivista della Civiltà Italiana* 5–6 (1998): 465–79, and "San Francesco in Petrarca ovvero, verso una semiologia francescana in Petrarca," in *San Francesco e il francescanesimo nella letteratura italiana dal XIII al XV secolo, Atti del Convegno Nazionale (Assisi, 10–12 dicembre 1999)*, ed. Stanislao Da Campagnola and Pasquale Tuscano (Assisi: Accademia Properziana del Subasio, 2001), 169–94.

75. Of the fifteen, Francis composed thirteen. The other two are scriptural Psalms 69 and 12 cited in their entirety. Each hour begins with an antiphon to the Virgin Mary followed by a psalm and a final blessing. See Francesco d'Assisi, *Scritti*, ed. Aristide Cabassi (Padua: Edizioni francescane, 2002), 153–99. On Francis's *Office*, see Rachel Fulton Brown, "Exegesis, Mimesis, and the Voice of Christ in Francis of Assisi's *Office of the Passion*," *Medieval Journal* 4.2 (2014): 39–62.

76. "pulso huc illuc corpuscolo collisione hominum." *De vita solitaria*, ed. Guido Martellotti (Turin: Einaudi, 1977), 170–73.

77. *Fam.* 10.4.28: "media autem nocte propter matutinam psalmodiam que illo presertim tempore in ecclesiis vestris auditur." *Le familiari*, 2:308; *Letters on Familiar Matters*, 2:74. Worth recalling is the fact that on his second trip to

liv Introduction

Naples, during which he witnessed the famous 1343 earthquake and tsunami, what he described, in *Fam.* 5.5.8–9, as a "storm without equal," Petrarch was staying with the Franciscans at San Lorenzo, "qui ex more ad nocturnas Cristi laudes surgebant" (who regularly used to rise for the nocturnal adoration of Christ). Petrarch writes that during that frightful night, "Omnes inde ad ecclesiam pergimus, ibique affusi multis cum gemitibus pernoctamus, cum iamiam adfuturum finem et ruitura circum omnia crederemus" (We then all proceeded to the church, and there we spent the night prostrate with much wailing, believing that our end was imminent). *Le familiari*, 2:16; *Letters on Familiar Matters*, 1:244–45.

78. References to the Psalms are according to the Septuagint-Vulgate numbering scheme, followed, in parenthesis, by the Hebrew numbering scheme (used by most modern editions of the Bible).

79. According to tradition, Augustine, on his deathbed, had them placed before him to read. See Driscoll, "The Seven Penitential Psalms," 154; Costley King'oo, *Miserere Mei*, 4–5.

80. However, Origen (d. ca. 254) had already noted the "penitential" connotation of the Psalms for Christians. See Driscoll, "The Seven Penitential Psalms," 153–55.

81. *Fam.* 10.5.28: "Ita michi placuit illud Psalmiste: 'Septies in die laudem dixi tibi,' ut ex quo semel hunc morem sum amplexus, nulla me vel semel ab incepto occupatio diurna distraxerit." *Le familiari*, 2:317; *Letters on Familiar Matters*, 2:81. It's worth noting that the sentence immediately following this one deals with lust: "Tertium est quod consortium femine, sine quo interdum extimaveram non posse vivere, morte nunc gravius pertimesco, et quanquam sepe tentationibus turber acerrimis, tamen dum in animum redit quid est femina, omnis tentatio confestim avolat et ego ad libertatem et ad pacem meam redeo" (Thirdly, I now fear more than death the company of women, without which I once thought I could not live. Although I am often disturbed by strong temptations, nevertheless upon recalling woman's nature, I feel every temptation immediately disappear and I return to my freedom and peace).

82. "sub nocte videbis Psallere pastorem!" *Petrarch's Bucolicum Carmen*, 9.

83. Cassian in reality was against the practice (soon to become normative in the West) of singing the *Gloria Patri* after each psalm. He claimed that the *Gloria* should be intoned only after singing all the psalms: "Illud etiam quod in hac prouincia uidimus, ut uno cantante in clausula psalmi omnes adstantes concinant cum clamore 'gloria Patri et Filio et Spiritui sancto', nusquam per omnem Orientem audiuimus, sed cum omnium silentio ab eo, qui cantat, finito psalmo orationem succedere, hac uero glorificatione Trinitatis tantummodo solere antiphona terminari" (Moreover, something that we observed in this country, which we have

not heard anywhere throughout the whole East, is that after one sings the closing of a psalm, all those present join in with a loud "Glory be to the Father, and to the Son, and to the Holy Spirit." Yet, unlike this practice, in other places, after the cantor finishes the psalm, everyone remains silent, and only then does this [hymn] glorifying the Trinity usually conclude the whole psalmody). Cassian, *Institutes* 2.8, SC 109, 72.

84. However, it could also trace back to Cassiodorus (490–585)—the first to single out the seven scriptural Psalms for their penitential dimension—for whom the number seven had a mystical significance: just as there are seven deadly sins, there are seven ways to make up for them: baptism, martyrdom, almsgiving, forgiving the sins of others, undergoing conversion, exhibiting Christian charity, and penance. On seven as a mystical number, see Driscoll, "The Seven Penitential Psalms," 161. On the philological, historical, and theological origins of the Gloria Patri, see especially Nicholas Ayo, C.S.C., *Gloria Patri* (Notre Dame, IN: University of Notre Dame Press, 2007).

85. On Petrarch's *Memoriale* and the use of "heu," see note 25.

86. Martinez, "Places and Times," 327–28.

87. Readers familiar with the *Rvf.*—characterized by the dichotomy-prone (and irresolute) architecture of both individual poems and larger sequences—will recognize in Petrarch's psalms the same recurring juxtaposition of contradictory feelings as well as the expression of conflictual and opposing themes. Just as the Petrarchan self is left dangerously fluctuating between sensual and spiritual love without resolution in the *Rvf.*, the same state of indecision and fragmentation emerges in the psalms: salvation, the arrival at a tranquil port, is a possibility that can be desired and sought after but never certain or achieved. On this crucial aspect of Petrarch's poetics, see in particular the essays in Michelangelo Picone, *Il Canzoniere: Lettura micro e macrotestuale* (Ravenna: Longo, 2007); and Mazzotta, *The World of Petrarch*, 58–79.

88. On a stylistic level, the frequent use of the *cursus velox* in psalm 4, highlighting the verbs of creation as a sign of God's power and goodness, echoes the Poverello's frequent use of the *velox* in the *Canticle* to convey the same ideals of harmony and beauty of creation. See Gianfranco Contini, "Un'ipotesi sulle *Laudes creaturarum*," in *Varianti e altra linguistica* (Turin: Einaudi, 1970), 141–59; and more recently, Pietrobon, "*Tam efficaciter utinam quam inculte*," 62.

89. Strong allusions to Cicero's *De natura deorum*, Ovid's *Metamorphoses*, and Horace's *Odes* are particularly present in this psalm. See Gigliucci, *Salmi penitenziali*, 12; and Ariani, *Petrarca*, 130.

90. Scholars have proposed various interpretations of the ways in which Petrarch's overall structure echoes the traditional arrangement of the seven

penitential Psalms. Giovanni Pozzi has suggested a sequence that mirrors the thematic structure of the traditional seven. In his reading, Petrarch's psalms 1 and 5 are about being shipwrecked and forsaken; psalms 2 and 6 focus on repentance and reconciliation with God; and psalms 3 and 7 instead highlight God's forgiveness. Pozzi's proposed structure is, therefore, perfectly symmetrical: a-b-c-d-a-b-c. By also focusing on the structure of the traditional seven Psalms, Matter points out how Pozzi's proposed framework is similar but also different from the traditional arrangement. In the latter, in fact, we can discern an overarching threefold structure where each group invokes God with specific requests: (1) Psalms 6, 31 (32), and 37 (38) address God, essentially saying, "don't be angry"; (2) Psalm 50 (51) articulates "have mercy"; and (3) Psalms 101 (102), 129 (130), and 142 (143) cry "hear me." In turn, these three groups reveal a further subdivision in an "a-b-a" sequence as the first and third Psalm of the first and third group begin with the same phrase: *Domine, ne in furore tuo arguas me* (Pss. 6 and 37 (38)) and *Domine, exaudi orationem mea* (Pss. 101 (102) and 142 (143)). The pattern, therefore, in this case is aba-c-aba. Thus both structures emphasize the central Psalm in each sequence. And it is here that the major differences between the traditional structure and Petrarch's come to light. If in fact the moving centerpiece in the traditional arrangement is the majestic *Miserere*, a Psalm of contrition and repentance, in Petrarch's arrangement we find an unexpected humanistic take on a psalm of praise. As Martinez has argued, this does not, however, weaken the relevance of the penitential sentiment of the *Miserere* since Petrarch's first psalm not only begins and ends with a similar cry, *Heu michi misero*, but the penitential element defines Petrarch's entire series. Martinez also observes how Petrarch's cry to be saved from his moral abyss recalls the Office of the Dead and the tradition of Christ's descent into and rescue of the just from Hell. See Pozzi, "Petrarca, i Padri e soprattutto la Bibbia," 164; Matter, "Petrarch's Personal Psalms," 225–26; Martinez, "Places and Times," 328.

91. "ut eos non tamquam a Propheta compositos, sed velut a se editos, quasi orationem propriam profunda cordis compunctione depromat, vel certe ad suam personam aestimet eos fuisse directos, eorumque sententias non tunc tantummodo per Prophetam aut in Propheta fuisse completas, sed in se quotidie geri implerique cognoscat. . . . Omnes namque hos affectus in Psalmis invenimus expressos, ut ea quae incurrerint, velut in speculo purissimo pervidentes, efficacius agnoscamus, et ita magistrantibus effectibus eruditi, non ut audita, sed tamquam perfecta palpemus, nec tamquam memoriae commendata, sed velut ipsi rerum naturae insita, de interno cordis parturiamus affectu, ut eorum sensus non textu lectionis, sed experientia praecedente penetremus, atque ita ad illam orationis incorruptionem mens nostra perveniat." The Latin text is from PL 49, 0838A–0839A.

The English translation is from Cassian, *Conference Ten on Prayer* (New York: Paulist Press, 1985), 137–38.

92. Regarding Jerome's translation, in *Fam.* 10.4.6–7, Petrarch notes, "Psalterium ipsum daviticum, quod die noctuque canitis, apud Hebreos metro constat, ut non immerito neque ineleganter hunc Cristianorum poetam nuncupare ausim; quippe quod et res ipsa suggerit et, si nichil hodie michi sine teste crediturus es, idem video sensisse Ieronimum, quamvis sacrum illud poema quod beatum virum, scilicet Cristum, canit nascentem morientem descendentem ad inferos resurgentem ascendentem reversurum, in aliam linguam simul sententia numerisque servatis transire nequiverit" (Jerome felt similarly, although he proved incapable of translating into another tongue, while retaining its meaning and meter, that sacred poem which sings of the birth, death, descent into Hell, resurrection, and return of that blessed man, Christ. He therefore concentrated on reproducing its meaning, yet even now it possesses a metrical quality, which causes us to call those lines of the Psalms verses). *Le familiari*, 2:302–3; *Letters on Familiar Matters*, 2:70.

93. "Semper habet lacrimas et pectore raucus anelat." *Petrarch's Bucolicum Carmen*, 10–11.

94. "penetransque animos dulcore latenti." *Petrarch's Bucolicum Carmen*, 12–13.

95. See Pozzi, "Petrarca, i Padri e soprattutto la Bibbia," 166.

96. *Fam.* 10.4.20: "secundi autem quia cum unum ex Cyclopibus Monicum dicant quasi monoculum, id quodam respectu proprie tibi convenire visum est, qui e duobus oculis, quibus omnes comuniter utimur mortales, quorum altero scilicet celestia altero terrena respicimus, tu terrena cernentem abiecisti oculo meliore contentus." *Le familiari*, 2:306; *Letters on Familiar Matters*, 2:72–73. On the monastic origins of the name, see Pozzi, "Petrarca, i Padri e soprattutto la Bibbia," 163.

97. The Gallican Psalter largely adheres to the concept of lines, stanzas, and literary elements found in the Septuagint, as "Hebraized" by the hexaplaric additions (and occasional changes). On the other hand, Jerome's "Hebrew Psalter" (*iuxta Hebraicum*) sometimes divides the lines differently, based on his understanding of the Hebrew text, often informed by the Greek translations of Aquila, Symmachus, and "Theodotion." Put simply, Jerome's Psalter may not read like traditional poetry, but it is structured and organized in poetic lines.

98. Widely used since antiquity, the *cursus*, that is, the practice of ending clauses and sentences with accentual rhythms, was a common stylistic device to enhance the harmony of Latin prose. The use varied throughout the High Middle Ages, but during the twelfth century, particularly in Italy and France, it went

through a process of simplification and, once adopted by the papal chancery, became known as *Cursus Curiae Romanae*. The so-called Roman system was taught by professors of *dictamen* including Guido Faba (d. ca. 1240) whose method became widespread. The Roman *cursus* was favored by authors outside papal chanceries and soon became standard throughout Europe; it influenced the writing of official Latin prose for centuries. The traditional rhythms of the Roman *cursus* were the *planus* (two unaccented syllables between the two accents and one unaccented syllable after the last accent; e.g., *vìncla perfrègit*), the *tardus* (two unaccented syllables both between the word accents and after the last; e.g., *vìncla perfrègerat*), and the *velox* (four unaccented syllables between the word accents and one after the last accent; e.g., *vìnculum fregeràmus*). Petrarchan scholars have analyzed the occurrence of *cursus* in Petrarch's Latin works, particularly in the *Rerum familiarum libri* and the *De viris illustribus*, where the incidence is high. For his psalms, Petrarch also adopted the *cursus trispondaicus*, which is normally formed by a polysyllabic and quadrisyllabic word both of which are stressed on the penultimate syllable (on the model of Cicero's *ésse videátur*). The most evident implication of Petrarch's use of the *cursus* is that his *devotiuncula*, far from being *inculte* (unrefined), as Petrarch had claimed in *Sen.* 10.1.132, is the result of a more elaborate and sophisticated compositional process than what Petrarch wanted us to believe. His careful attention to the rhythm and placement of words in composing the psalms could also suggest that they were intended to be read aloud—just as the epistolary prose for which *cursus* was formulated in the late twelfth and early thirteenth century—or at least, even when read silently, to adhere to rules intended to enhance the harmony and effectiveness of Latin prose, a practice already detectible in patristic homilies, letters, and commentaries as well as early liturgical prayers and texts. For a general treatment of *cursus*, with illustrative cases and bibliography, see F. A. C. Mantello and A. G. Rigg, eds., *Medieval Latin: An Introduction and Bibliographical Guide* (Washington, DC: Catholic University of America Press, 1966), 111–21; Tore Janson, *Prose Rhythm in Medieval Latin from the 9th to the 13th Century* (Stockholm: Almqvist & Wiksell International, 1975); S. M. Oberhelman, "The History and Development of the *Cursus Mixtus* in Latin Literature," *Classical Quarterly* 38.1 (1988): 228–42. On Petrarch's use of *cursus*, see Witt, *In the Footsteps of the Ancients*, 230–91; Guido Martellotti, "Clausole e ritmi nella prosa narrativa del Petrarca," in Feo and Rizzo, *Guido Martellotti: Scritti petrarcheschi*, 207–19. A more recent and detailed analysis of *cursus* in Petrarch's seven psalms is provided in Pietrobon, "*Tam efficaciter utinam quam inculte*," 61–65.

99. "cum te suspiriis sanctis ac piis lacrimis, quibus ad frangendam peccati duritiem iramque Dei leniendem atque avertendam et gratiam consequendam nichil est efficacius." *Res seniles*, 3:142; *Letters of Old Age*, 2:358.

100. The most comprehensive and influential study to date of Petrarch's prayers is Donatella Coppini, "Le preghiere del Petrarca," in *Estravaganti, Disperse, Apocrifi Petrarcheschi*, ed. Claudia Barra and Paola Vecchi Galli (Milan: Cisalpino, 2006), 595–612. See also Coppini's other essays on the topic: "Adonay domine deus: Preghiere attribuite a Petrarca nella tradizione manoscritta," *Quaderni petrarcheschi* 17–18 (2007–8): 1139–60; and "Preghiere," in Feo, *Petrarca nel tempo*, 446–54.

101. See *Sen.* 10.2.72: "Quotiens per estate media nocte surrexerim et, nocturnis Christo laudibus persolutis" (how often I rise in the middle of the night throughout the summer, and, after reciting the nightly office in praise of Christ). *Res seniles*, 3:162; *Letters of Old Age*, 2:365.

102. *Fam.* 5.5.19, addressed to Cardinal Colonna, ends with the following words: "hoc unum michi certe prestiterit, ut te obsecrem ne me unquam amplius vitam ventis ac fluctibus credere iubeas. Hoc enim est in quo neque tibi neque Romano Pontifici neque patri meo, si ad lucem redeat, parere velim. Aerem volucribus, mare piscibus relinquo; terrenum animal, terrestre iter eligo. Dum pes meus terram calcet, nec pharetratum Sarmatam, nec ludentem in hospitibus Maurum adire renuo; mitte me quo vis" (There is one thing I want to be certain does emerge: that is, I beseech you not ever again to order me to place my trust in winds and seas. This is something in which I would obey neither you, the pope, nor my own father if he were to return to life. I shall leave the air to the birds and the sea to the fish; as a terrestrial animal I shall prefer land trips. *As long as my foot treads the ground, I will not refuse to go to a quivered Sarmatian, or a Moor playing among his guests; send me where you will* [translation in italics mine]). *Le familiari*, 2:19; *Letters on Familiar Matters*, 1:247. This decision may explain Petrarch's refusal to accept the invitation from his friend Giovanni Mandelli to go on a pilgrimage to the Holy Land. However, he eventually presented Mandelli with a pilgrimage guide, the *Itinerarium ad sepulchrum domini nostri Jesu Christi*. See Theodore J. Cachey Jr., *Petrarch's Guide to the Holy Land* (Notre Dame, IN: University of Notre Dame Press, 2002); and "*Peregrinus* (quasi) ubique: Petrarca e la storia del viaggio," *Intersezioni* 27 (1997): 369–84.

103. *Fam.* 22.10.11: "Quos inter merito michi maximus David semper fuerit, eo formosior quo incomptior, eo doctior disertiorque quo purior" (For me the greatest in terms of merit will always be David, who is the more beautiful for his simplicity, the more learned for his purity). *Le familiari*, 4:128; *Letters on Familiar Matters*, 3:233.

A NOTE ON THE TRANSLATION

In *Epistle* 106.29.2, on translating the Psalms, Jerome writes, "We should not translate word for words in such a way that, while we adhere to the syllable, we lose the meaning."[1] Jerome thus argues for a translation that is idiomatic rather than word for word, one that understands the particular idiom of the source language and does not "damage" the sense while recasting it in the particular idiom of the receptor language. Jerome's approach to translation has certainly not lost its relevance and validity. Heeding his advice, I have tried to remain as faithful as possible to Petrarch's original text while also striving to produce a readable version in clear and idiomatic English. Moreover, although there is a deliberate attempt on the part of Petrarch to reproduce the uncultivated "vox rauca" (hoarse voice) of the Davidic style and emulate the prose-like verses of the Psalms in Jerome's Latin rendering, my translation, while respecting the verse structure and line breaks of the original, focuses primarily on rendering the sense of the original text without attempting to re-create any particular style or prose, be it poetic or rhythmic.

The text of Petrarch's psalms and prayers I have used is the one established by Donatella Coppini for the edition of the centenary published by Le Lettere in Florence in 2010. I have adopted American-style punctuation when necessary. Any divergence from Coppini's edition, such as minor style adjustments, other spellings, and variants worth citing from other editions, is acknowledged in the notes.

In general, the notes are designed to aid understanding of the text and provide relevant information to recover the historical and cultural context in which Petrarch's seven psalms and prayers were written. More importantly, given the highly specific and subtle allusions to the canonical Psalms, other religious or classical sources, as well as Petrarch's other works, I refer readers to this material as well. The notes rely heavily on the valuable and informative commentaries by Marino Casali, Henry Cochin, Donatella Coppini, and Roberto Gigliucci.[2]

NOTES

1. Graves, *Jerome, Epistle 106 (on the Psalms)*, 57.
2. Marino Casali, "Petrarca 'Penitenziale': Dai Salmi alle Rime," *Lettere italiane* 20.3 (1968): 366–82; and "Imitazione e ispirazione nei 'Salmi penitenziali' del Petrarca," *Studi petrarcheschi* 7 (1961): 151–70; Henry Cochin, *Pétrarque: Les Psaumes Pénitentiaux publiés d'après le manuscrit de la Bibliothèque de Lucerne; préf. de Pierre de Nolhac* (Paris: L. Rouart, 1929); Coppini, *Psalmi penitentiales; Orationes*; Gigliucci, *Salmi penitenziali*, 60–81.

PETRARCH'S SEVEN PSALMS

Francisci Petrarce laureati septem psalmi penitentiales incipiunt feliciter

Psalmus I

1. Heu michi misero, quia iratum adversus me constitui redemptorem meum et legem suam contumaciter neglexi.
2. Iter rectum sponte deserui et per invia longe lateque circumactus sum.
3. Aspera quelibet et inaccessa penetravi, et ubique labor et angustie.
4. Unus aut alter ex gregibus brutorum, et inter lustra ferarum habitatio mea.
5. In anxietatibus cum voluptate versatus sum et in sentibus cubile meum stravi.
6. Et obdormivi in interitum et speravi requiem in tormentis.
7. Nunc igitur quid agam? Quo me in tantis periculis vertam? Spes adolescentie mee corruerunt omnes.
8. Et factus sum naufrago simillimus, qui, mercibus amissis, nudus enatat, iactatus ventis et pelago.
9. Elongatus ego sum a portu et viam salutis non apprehendo, sed rapior sinistrorsum.
10. Video tenuiter quidem, sed hinc michi gravius duellum, quia irascor michimet et anime mee sum infestus.
11. Irascor peccatis meis, sed ingenti miseriarum mole depressus sum, nec est respirandi locus.
12. Sepe fugam retentavi et vetustum iugum excutere meditatus sum, sed inheret ossibus.
13. O si tandem excidat a collo meo! Excidet confestim, si tu iusseris, altissime.
14. O si michi sic irascar ut te diligam, vel sero!
15. Sed multum timeo, quia libertas mea meis manibus labefacta est.
16. Iuste crucior: consensi. Labore torqueor dignissimo.

The seven penitential psalms of [poet] laureate Francesco Petrarca duly begin

Psalm I

1. Oh, wretched me,[1] for I have made my Redeemer angry at me and obstinately I scorned his law![2]
2. I have left the right path of my own will,[3] and far and wide I have wandered[4] in desolate places.
3. I have penetrated every harsh and inaccessible place,[5] with toil and anguish at every turn.
4. I was just one among many in the herds of brutes, and my dwelling was among the dens of beasts.[6]
5. In anxieties, with pleasure,[7] I wallowed and spread my bed among thorns.[8]
6. And I slept in my downfall[9] and hoped to find rest among torments.
7. So, what do I do now?[10] Where do I turn in such great dangers? The hopes of my youth[11] have all vanished.
8. And I have become like a shipwreck[12] who has lost his goods and swims exposed, battered by the winds and the sea.
9. I have strayed from the port[13] and I do not take the path of salvation, instead I am pulled away to the wrong side.[14]
10. I see acutely,[15] but this is why my struggle is more severe,[16] for I am angry at myself and am an enemy to my soul.
11. I am angry because of my sins, but I am crushed by the enormous amount of my miseries,[17] and there is no way to breathe.
12. Several times I tried to escape,[18] and I thought about shaking off the ancient yoke,[19] but it is attached to my bones.
13. Oh, if it would finally fall from my neck! It will at once, Most High, if you command it.
14. Oh, if only I could get angry with myself so much to love you, even if it is late!
15. But I fear greatly, because I have destroyed my freedom with my own hands.[20]
16. Rightly I am tormented: I consented. My toil is richly deserved.

17. Quid michi procuravi, demens? Cathenam meam ipse contexui et incidi volens in insidias mortis.
18. Retia michi disposuit hostis quacumque ibam et pedibus meis laqueos tetendit.
19. Ego autem despexi et incessi securus inter lubrica et in peccatis michi blanditus sum.
20. Credidi iuventutis decus aberrare et secutus sum qua me tulit impetus.
21. Et dixi mecum: quid ante medium de extremis cogitas? Habet etas quelibet suos fines.
22. Videt ista Deus, sed irridet. Facillimus erit ad veniam. Converti poteris cum voles.
23. Nunc consuetudo pessima suum vendicat mancipium et inicit manus frustra reluctanti.
24. Quo fugiam non habeo: nam et ego vinctus sum et refugium meum longe est.
25. Moriar in peccatis meis, nisi auxilium michi veniat ex alto.
26. Non merui, fateor: sed tu, Domine, miserere, et extende manum pereunti.
27. Et, memor promissionum tuarum, eripe me de faucibus inferni.
28. Gloria Patri et Filio et Spiritui Sancto. Sicut erat in principio et nunc et semper et in secula seculorum. Amen.

Psalmus II

1. Invocabo quem offendi, nec timebo. Revocabo quem abieci, nec erubescam.
2. Spem perditam restituam. Audebo rursum ex his tenebris in celum oculos attollere.
3. Illic habitat redemptor meus, qui potens est ab inferis evellere
4. et gelidis artubus spiritum infundere et extrahere iacentem de sepulcro.
5. Ego in me perii, sed in illo vita michi permanet et salus in eternum.
6. Ille imperat morti, ille vitam prestat et restaurat. Quis prohibet sperare meliora?
7. Avolent qui me terrificant. Peccatum meum grande nimis, sed miseratio Domini immensa est.

17. What did I do to myself, fool that I am? I forged my own chain and voluntarily I have fallen into the snares of death.
18. The enemy prepared nets wherever I went and stretched snares for my feet.[21]
19. But I did not concern myself and advanced with confidence toward dangerous places[22] and in my sins I flattered myself.
20. I thought it was fitting for my youth to abandon the right path,[23] and I followed my own instincts.
21. And I said to myself: why do you think about the end before even getting halfway? Every age has its limits.
22. God sees all this but mocks me.[24] He will be very willing to forgive. You can repent when you so desire.
23. Now the debasing habit[25] claims its slave and claims the possession of those who uselessly resist.[26]
24. I have no place to escape: I am tied up and my refuge is far away.
25. I will die in my sins, if I do not get help from above.
26. I did not deserve it, I confess: but you, Lord, have mercy,[27] and stretch out your hand to me as I die.
27. And mindful of your promises, snatch me from the jaws of hell.[28]
28. Glory be to the Father, and to the Son, and to the Holy Spirit, as it was in the beginning, is now, and ever shall be, world without end. Amen.

Psalm II

1. I will call on the one I have rejected, and I will not fear. I will call again on the one whom I have cast off, nor will I be ashamed.[29]
2. I will recover the lost hope. I will still dare to raise from this darkness my eyes to heaven.
3. There lives my redeemer, who has the power to rescue from the abyss
4. and breathe life into cold limbs and bring the dead out from the tomb.[30]
5. In myself I have perished, but in him I still have life and salvation forever.
6. He rules over death, he gives and renews life. Who forbids to hope for better?
7. May those who threaten me disappear. My sin is too great, but the Lord's mercy is immeasurable.

8. Peccavi, infelix, mala peioribus accumulans et michimet hostis acerrimus.
9. Verum enimvero omnes sordes meas una gutta vel tenuis sacri sanguinis absterget.
10. Attamen unde michi gemitus, frange saxum hoc, Domine, et fontes proruant ex adamante durissimo!
11. Fontes limpidi scaturiant et descendant in volutabrum ubi assidue trux aper immergitur.
12. Et diluantur macule vetuste, ut placere tibi possit habitaculum in me, dum michi displicet.
13. Fiat michi pernox miseriarum mearum recordatio et per diem spes salutis appareat.
14. Temperem leta cum tristibus, sed miserationum tuarum nunquam obliviscar:
15. ex quantis me malis erueris et ut animam meam non deserueris in periculis multis.
16. Lugeam penitens de commissis, ad feliciora suspirem. De me ipso metuam semper, de te nunquam desperem.
17. Fiat michi thalamus meus purgatorium meum et lectulus meus lacrimarum conscius mearum.
18. Et in corpore meo doleam, priusquam preceps corruam in Tartara.
19. Miserere, Domine, miserere, et opus tuum ne destituas, liberator meus et spes ultima!
20. Gloria Patri et Filio et Spiritui Sancto. Sicut erat in principio et nunc et semper et in secula seculorum. Amen.

Psalmus III

1. Miserere dolorum meorum, Domine. Satis superque volutatus sum et in ceno peccatorum meorum marcui miser.
2. Et quid restat amplius afflicto? Tempus inutiliter abiit. Vitam in consiliis expendi.
3. Mors ante oculos meos adest, et domus novissima sepulcrum et stridor ac gemitus gehenne.

8. I have sinned, wretched that I am, adding bad to worse,[31] and a fierce enemy to myself I have become.
9. But in truth a single drop, even small, of the sacred blood will wash away all my filth.[32]
10. However, this rock from which my laments come, you, Lord, break it and may springs come forth from the hardest stone![33]
11. May clear springs gush and pour into the marsh where the wild boar continues to plunge.[34]
12. And let the ancient stains be washed away, so that you may be pleased to have a home in me,[35] where I myself would not want to live.
13. Let the memory of my miseries last for me all night long and with the day may the hope of salvation appear.[36]
14. Let me mitigate joy with sadness,[37] but may I never forget your acts of mercy.
15. From how many evils you have rescued me and how you have not forsaken my soul amidst many dangers.
16. Let me weep from regret for what I have done, and sigh for a happier life. Let me fear myself, while never despairing of you.[38]
17. Let my bedroom become my purgatory and may my little bed be the witness to my tears.[39]
18. And let me feel pain in my body, before falling headfirst into Tartarus.
19. Have mercy, Lord, have mercy, and do not forsake your creature, O my deliverer and only hope![40]
20. Glory be to the Father, and to the Son, and to the Holy Spirit, as it was in the beginning, is now, and ever shall be, world without end. Amen.

Psalm III

1. Have mercy on my afflictions, Lord. More than enough have I wallowed, languishing in the filth of my sins.[41]
2. What else is left to me in my affliction? Time has gone by uselessly.[42] I spent my life in [vain] deliberations.[43]
3. Death appears before my eyes,[44] and so does the tomb, our last home, and the howling and wailing of Gehenna.[45]

4. Quam diu me deludet hodiernus dies sub expectatione crastini? Quando incipiam ad te reverti?
5. Siste iam fluctus ac procellas animi. Illumina consilium cordis mei et metam laboribus impone.
6. Qui intellectum dederas ut bene agerem, tribue voluntatem et in actum dirige, ne exprobratione tui muneris confundar.
7. Eripe me servitio hostis tui et ne insultet in opus manuum tuarum prohibe, quoniam alter qui prohibeat non est.
8. Libera me de suppliciis eternis. Sit michi pars purgationis labor meus, quo hic per singulos dies exerceor.
9. Reliquum in hac vita et in his membris exige, priusquam veniat tempus egestatis.
10. Reduc me in vias tuas ante solis occasum. Advesperascit enim, et nox est amica predonibus.
11. Coge me ad te, si vocare parum est. Denique ut libet, modo ne peream.
12. Respice, Domine, vide, miserere, succurre, quoniam tu solus omnes miserias meas nosti.
13. Gloria Patri et Filio et Spiritui Sancto. Sicut erat in principio et nunc et semper et in secula seculorum. Amen.

Psalmus IV

1. Recordari libet munerum tuorum, Deus, ut sit michi confusio ante oculos et rubor in genis meis.
2. Sic enim forte misereberis, ubi non prorsus oblitum videris omnium que michi tribuisti, largitor optime.
3. Tu michi celum et stellas (quid enim horum indigebas?), tu michi vicissitudines temporum creasti.
4. Tu solem et lunam, tu dies noctesque, tu lucem ac tenebras discrevisti.
5. Aer opus est digitorum tuorum, serenitatem et nubes tu fecisti et ventos et pluvias.
6. Terram aquis involvisti, fecisti montes et maria, valles ac planiciem, fontes, lacus et flumina.

4. How long will I be fooled by the present in waiting for tomorrow?[46] When will I begin to return to you?
5. Hold back the waves and the storms of the soul.[47] Enlighten the deliberation of my heart and put an end to my toil.
6. You who gave me the intellect to do well,[48] give me the resolve and direct me to action,[49] so that I am not confused by the reproach of your gift.
7. Save me from your enemy's bondage[50] and keep him from raging against the work of your hands,[51] for there is no one else to prevent him from doing so.[52]
8. Release me from the eternal torments. May my toil be part of my purgation, by which I am occupied every single day.[53]
9. Demand what is left in this life and in these limbs, before the time of want comes.[54]
10. Lead me back to your ways[55] before sunset. In fact, it is evening,[56] and the night is friendly to robbers.[57]
11. Compel me to you, if calling me is not enough. Finally, do as you please with me, as long as I do not perish.
12. Turn your eyes on me, Lord, see me, have mercy, rescue me, for you alone know all my miseries.[58]
13. Glory be to the Father, and to the Son, and to the Holy Spirit, as it was in the beginning, is now, and ever shall be, world without end. Amen.

Psalm IV

1. I like to remind myself of your gifts, Lord, so that there may be shame before my eyes and blushing on my cheeks.[59]
2. Perhaps you will then have mercy, O generous provider, when you see that I did not completely forget all that you have given me.
3. For me you created the sky and the stars (what need would you have had of them?), and the changes in the seasons.[60]
4. You have separated light from darkness;[61] sun and moon, days and nights.
5. The sky is the work of your hands,[62] you have created the fair weather and the clouds, the winds and the rains.
6. You surrounded the land with waters, you made the mountains and the seas, the valleys and the plains, the springs, the lakes, and the rivers.

7. Hec intus variis seminibus fecundasti, circum quoque multiplici specie decorasti.
8. Herbis virentibus vestisti campos, distinxisti colles floribus et silvas ramorum foliis.
9. Fatigato requiem preparasti, estuanti umbras arborum et ad otium recessus amenissimos,
10. sitienti fontes lucidos, esurienti baccas omnis generis et refectionis quam multiplicis alimenta.
11. Quam multiformibus animantibus terras et pelagus implesti, et circumfusos tractus aeris! Quis cuncta dinumeret?
12. Hec omnia pedibus hominis subiecisti: usque ad oblectationes varias amasti hominem.
13. Nec me minus ideo quia cum multis: quin et singularia quedam prebuisti michi.
14. Tu corpus hominis pre cunctis creaturis tuis adornasti, tu membra miris ordinibus collocasti.
15. Os illi imperiosum ac serenum spiritumque tui capacem et contemplatorem celestium statuisti.
16. Addidisti artes innumeras quibus vita hec foret ornatior, eterne quoque vite spem dedisti.
17. Ostendisti viam qua gradiendum foret. Aperuisti aditum in tabernacula tua. Monuisti quid cavendum atque unde declinandum sit.
18. Deputasti comitem perpetuum ac ducem. Gressus omnes e specula contemplatus es et errores meos observasti.
19. Cadentem sustentasti, labentem firmasti, errantem direxisti, prostratum sustulisti, suscitasti mortuum.
20. Miseratus es labores meos totiens ubi non misericordia sed odio dignus eram.
21. Et quibus meis meritis tam multa, tam grandia? Gratis et indignus hec accepi.
22. Pro his omnibus quid tibi retribuerim vides. Verumtamen miserere iterum et succurre, quia sine te morior.

7. These you have fertilized with various seeds, and all around you have adorned them with numerous beauties.
8. You have covered the fields with green grasses, you have decorated the hills with flowers and the woods with the leaves of the branches.
9. To those who are tired you have offered respite, to those who are burning hot the shade of the trees, and very pleasant hideaways to rest,
10. to the thirsty [you have offered] limpid waters,[63] to the hungry fruits of all kinds, and the most various food as nourishment.
11. With how many species of living beings have you filled the earth and the sea, and the vastness of the sky all around! Who could count them all?
12. You have put all these at human's feet:[64] so much as to give them to humans as pleasures.
13. And no less did you love me because you loved me with many others: for indeed you gave me unique gifts.[65]
14. You have adorned humans' body above all your creatures,[66] you have arranged their limbs in a marvelous order.[67]
15. You have shaped their powerful and serene face and have made their spirit capable of comprehending you and contemplating heavenly goods.[68]
16. You have added countless arts to make this life more beautiful,[69] and you have given us the hope of eternal life.
17. You showed us the path to take.[70] You have opened for us an access to your tabernacles.[71] You warned us what to beware of and what to stay away from.
18. You gave us a companion and a guide forever.[72] From on high you have watched all my steps[73] and have noticed my mistakes.
19. You supported me when I fell,[74] you held me tight when I wavered, you showed me the way when I wandered, you lifted me up when I was down, you raised me when I was dead.
20. You had compassion for my toils so many times, when I deserved not your mercy but your hatred.[75]
21. And for what merits of mine so many and great gifts? I received them freely and unworthily.[76]
22. For all these gifts, see what I gave you in return. However, have mercy again and rescue me, because without you I perish.

Psalmus V

23. Ingratitudinum mearum ne reminiscaris amplius, sed salvam fac animam meam, nil iam de propriis viribus sperantem.
24. Gloria Patri et Filio et Spiritui Sancto. Sicut erat in principio et nunc et semper et in secula seculorum. Amen.

Psalmus V

1. Noctes mee in merore transeunt et terroribus agitant innumeris. Conscientia concutit insomnem et male michi est.
2. Somnus meus illusionibus variis turbatur, non michi quietem afferens, sed laborem.
3. Signum pestiferi eventus prohibe, Domine, et occurre, quoniam adventantis mortis est indicium.
4. Dies meos in amaritudinibus exegi, consumpserunt me cure immortales et anime mee litigio exasperatus sum.
5. Corporis mei sarcina defessus ac curvatus ingredior et terram invitus aspicio.
6. Intus et extra michi ipse sum molestus. Utrobique hostes domesticos inveni, qui me pessundederunt.
7. Persecutoribus alienigenis patuit ingressus et murorum custodia deiecta est.
8. Et ego, somno gravis atque incautus, inter tenebras noctis oppressus sum.
9. Nulla michi spes salutis, nullum presidium aliunde, sed in misericordia tua, Domine, sperabo.
10. Succurre, accelera, fer opem et miserere mei.
11. Gloria Patri et Filio et Spiritui Sancto. Sicut erat in principio et nunc et semper et in secula seculorum. Amen.

Psalmus VI

1. Circumvallarunt me inimici mei, perurgentes me cuspide multiplici.

23. My offenses, do not remember them anymore, but save my soul, which now no longer hopes in its strength.[77]
24. Glory be to the Father, and to the Son, and to the Holy Spirit, as it was in the beginning, is now, and ever shall be, world without end. Amen.

Psalm V

1. My nights drown in sadness and shake me with innumerable terrors. My conscience torments me; I am sleepless, and for me there is nothing but evil.
2. My sleep is troubled by various nightmares,[78] and brings no rest, but labor.
3. Hold back from me, O Lord, the sign of ruinous events, and come to my rescue, for it is an indication of the coming death.
4. In bitterness I spent my days,[79] undying troubles have consumed me, and I am tormented by the discord of my soul.
5. Weary and bent under the weight of my body,[80] I carry on and unwillingly keep my eyes low.
6. Inside and out I am a nuisance to myself. And inside and out I have found familiar enemies,[81] who have destroyed me.
7. The entrance has been opened to foreign persecutors, and the protection of the walls has been brought down.[82]
8. And I, weighed down by sleep and reckless, have been defeated in the darkness of the night.
9. I have no hope for salvation,[83] no help from anywhere else, but I will hope, Lord, in your mercy.[84]
10. Rescue me, make haste,[85] come to my aid and have mercy on me.
11. Glory be to the Father, and to the Son, and to the Holy Spirit, as it was in the beginning, is now, and ever shall be, world without end. Amen.

Psalm VI

1. My enemies surrounded me,[86] constantly pursuing me with their many spears.

2. Obtorpui infelix et contremui vehementer. Horror mortis superastitit michi.
3. Incubui in baculum meum et dixi: ecce perferam, nec succumbam.
4. Non respexi ad orientem, nec unde debueram auxilium expectavi, nec sicut dignum fuerat speravi.
5. Propterea firmamentum cui innixus eram me destituit repente et ego pronus in terram sum prostratus.
6. Agnovi cadens quam debiliter stetissem. Predones insultarunt corruenti;
7. spoliarunt me divitiis multis, quesitis michi de longinquo, tabe et cruore deformarunt me;
8. vulneribus gravissimis confecerunt me, semianimem ac nudum reliquerunt in deserto;
9. caput et pectus meum transfixerunt, sed subter precordia mea debachati sunt acerbius.
10. Illic vulnus situ putruit, illic vite mee metuo, illic, Domine, manus tuas adhibe velociter.
11. Vivis enim, salvator mi, et hec aspiciens ex alto tacuisti et passus es, quia ego promerui.
12. Misereberis fortasse, nec patieris in finem, quoniam tu solus potens es prescribere leges morti.
13. Ipse arcebis carnifices ab interitu meo, quoniam in te spes mea magna est. Ipse salvum me facies de manibus impiorum.
14. Gloria Patri et Filio et Spiritui Sancto. Sicut erat in principio et nunc et semper et in secula seculorum. Amen.

Psalmus VII

1. Cogitabam stare, dum corrui. Ve michi, quia duriter nimis allisus sum.
2. Quo et unde redactus sum, horresco dum memini et contremisco graviter.

2. I, a wretched man, became numb and trembled violently. The horror of death overwhelmed me.[87]
3. I leaned on my staff and said, "Here, I will carry through, I will not succumb."
4. I did not look to the east, nor did I expect help from where I should have expected it, nor did I hope, as it was right to do.
5. The support on which I had leaned gave way unexpectedly and I fell to the ground.[88]
6. Falling, I realized how infirmly I had been standing. As I fell, robbers attacked me;[89]
7. they stripped me of many riches, gathered from afar. They left me disfigured, broken, and in blood;
8. with the deepest wounds they finished me off, lifeless and naked they abandoned me in the desert.[90]
9. They pierced my head and my chest,[91] but more cruelly they raged under my heart.
10. The wound putrefied in neglect.[92] I fear for my life, Lord, quickly lay your hands on it.
11. You are the living God, my savior, and looking at these things from above,[93] you kept silent and let it happen, because I well deserved them.[94]
12. Perhaps you will have mercy, you will not allow it to the end,[95] because you alone have the power to impart laws to death.
13. You will ward off the executioners from my death, because in you my hope is great. You will save me from the hands of the wicked.[96]
14. Glory be to the Father, and to the Son, and to the Holy Spirit, as it was in the beginning, is now, and ever shall be, world without end. Amen.

Psalm VII

1. I thought I was standing firm, but I collapsed.[97] Woe to me, for I was completely shipwrecked![98]
2. I shudder when I remember where I led myself, and where I was, and I tremble all over.

3. Sperabam de viribus meis et michi quedam magna promiseram.
4. Somnia michi fingebam, et gaudebam. Nunc delusus expergiscor cum lacrimis.
5. Securus in periculis fui, letus in erumnis. Mediis portum in tempestatibus putavi.
6. Circumspexi per nebulas, secutus sum transversas et tortuosas vivendi vias, et infeliciter mulcentes.
7. Nosti quoniam tu semper michi fueras finis. Sed, ad te per me ipsum venire credens, retrocessi per inextricabiles anfractus.
8. Sentio nunc insidias ubilibet. Piget erroris tam longevi, nec propterea subsisto ubi sit requies.
9. Odio michi sum, et ago cuncta cum fastidio. Vim patior et aliud non licet.
10. Novum propositum mos vetustus opprimit et cum recta placuerint relabor ad solita.
11. Quotiens iam oscitans ad vomitum redii et subinde stomachans dixi: quousque hec, et quis erit finis?
12. Iustum supplicium animi insolentis! Scio quid me perdidit: nichil eram et supercilium erexi.
13. Agnosco nullam homini fiduciam nisi in Deo, et si parum video, illucescat clarius.
14. Aufer a me, Domine, presumptionis spiritum et humilitatem tribue placentem tibi,
15. nequando extollar inconsulte et michi de me mentiar, sed perseverem in tremore tuo.
16. Limus et umbra tenuis sum et fumus ante impetum ventorum: ita michi videor videri.
17. Ita michi videar semper et in hac opinione permaneam sobrie ac salubriter, sub umbra tua.
18. Quotiens hinc pedem movero, concidam et ludibrium persecutoribus meis ero.
19. Scio et expertus metuo: operuit me iam similis ruina.
20. Et adhuc exsurgere non valui, sed inenarrabilibus urgeor miseriis.

3. I trusted my strength and intended great things for myself.
4. I built dreams for myself, and I relished in them. Now, deluded, I wake up in tears.
5. I was free from care in dangers, happy in misfortunes. I thought I was in port when I was in the midst of storms.[99]
6. I searched in the mist;[100] I followed life paths twisted and tortuous, and mortally seductive.
7. You knew that you were always my goal. But, relying on my own to come to you, I went backward through twists and turns.[101]
8. Now I see pitfalls everywhere. I regret such a prolonged errancy, yet I do not rest where there is peace.
9. I hate myself,[102] and I do everything with disgust. I suffer violence and I'm helpless.[103]
10. The old habit crushes the new purpose and even though I chose righteousness, I fall back into my usual ways.[104]
11. How many times already have I idly returned to my vomit,[105] only to regret it immediately afterward and say: for how long, and how will it end?
12. A just punishment for an arrogant soul! I know what ruined me: I was nothing and I raised my eyebrows.[106]
13. I realize that man can trust no one except God, and if I see dimly,[107] may a brighter light shine.
14. Take away from me, Lord, the spirit of presumption and give me that humility you love,[108]
15. so that I may never rise inconsiderately and deceive myself,[109] but [that I may] continue to tremble in front of you.[110]
16. I am mud, a weak shadow, and smoke faced by the impetus of the winds:[111] thus I appear to myself.[112]
17. And may I always appear thus to myself, and may I remain in this opinion sensibly and wholesomely, in your shadow.[113]
18. Every time I move my foot from here, I will stumble and become the object of ridicule for my persecutors.[114]
19. I know it, and for having experienced it, I stand in fear of it: already a similar downfall has knocked me down.
20. And I still have not been able to rise up,[115] but I am oppressed by indescribable torments.

21. Tamdiu fedus versor in sanguinibus et in luto concupiscentiarum mearum iaceo.
22. Erige me, Criste Ihesu, et misericorditer sustenta, ne corruam sub extremis.
23. Gloria Patri et Filio et Spiritui Sancto. Sicut erat in principio et nunc et semper et in secula seculorum. Amen.

21. For a long time, I have been living wretchedly amid bloodshed,[116] and lying in the filth of my lustful acts.[117]
22. Lift me up, Christ Jesus, and hold me in your mercy, lest I collapse at my last end.[118]
23. Glory be to the Father, and to the Son, and to the Holy Spirit, as it was in the beginning, is now, and ever shall be, world without end. Amen.

Notes

Psalm I

1. *Heu* sets the tone and signals the distress and the confessional mode for the entire sequence while echoing the penitential psalm par excellence, Ps. 50 (51), the *Miserere*. References to the Psalms are according to the Septuagint-Vulgate numbering, followed, when necessary, by the standard Hebrew numbering in parentheses, the one used by most modern editions of the Bible.

2. Cassiodorus, *Expositio psalmorum*, 89.11: "si testamenta eius [Christi] contumaciter neglegamus" (if we stubbornly disregard his [Christ's] covenants). The Latin text is available at CC, https://www.mlat.uzh.ch/browser?path=1027&text=21404.

3. The two paths in life appear often, especially in *Rvf*.; see 68 "la via di salir al ciel" (the way to mount to heaven). The Italian text and English translation of *Rvf.* are from *Petrarch's Lyric Poems: The Rime Sparse and Other Lyrics*, trans. and ed. Robert M. Durling (Cambridge, MA: Harvard University Press, 1976), 148–49.

4. This line well encapsulates Petrarch's view of his entire life: "sic sum peregrinus ubique" (so I am a wanderer everywhere). *Ep. metr.* 3.19.16. The Latin text is from *Epistulae Metricae / Briefe in Versen*, ed. Otto Schönberger and Eva Schönberger (Würzburg: Königshausen & Neumann, 2004), 270.

5. In *Eclogue* 1.3, *Parthenias*, Silvius laments, "ast ego dumosos colles silvasque pererro" (I, hapless vagrant, go straying o'er thorny hills and through thickets). *Petrarch's Bucolicum Carmen*, 2–3.

6. Ps. 79.14 (80.13): "vastavit eam aper de silva" (The boar from the forest ravages it).

7. Worth noting here is the crucial combination of torment and pleasure in the Petrarchan introspective universe; the *atra voluptas* in the *Secretum* disobeys the Senecan warning: "Quid enim est turpius quam captare in ipso luctu voluptatem, immo per luctum, et inter lacrimas quoque quod iuvet quaerere?" (For what is baser than to 'chase after' pleasure in the very midst of mourning—nay rather by means of mourning—and even amid one's tears to hunt out that which will give pleasure? *Ep.* 99.26; Loeb translation). Enrico Fenzi also cites *Ad Marciam*, 1.7, in his commentary on the *Secretum* (Milan: Mursia, 1992), 344 n. 175 (all Latin citations from the *Secretum* are from this edition). As Casali observes, the fundamental themes of the *Secretum* are present in Petrarch's psalms, particularly in this first one: from the weakness of the will (the main one) to *acedia*; from self-satisfaction to confidence in one's own strength and in one's own future (Casali,

"Petrarca 'Penitenziale,'" 371–73). See also *De remediis*, 2.93, and related commentary in *Petrarch's Remedies for Fortune Fair and Foul*, 5 vols., trans. and comm. C. H. Rawski (Bloomington: Indiana University Press, 1991), 4:359. Francisco Rico, in *Vida u obra de Petrarca: Volumen 1: Lectura del "Secretum"* (Barcelona: Ariel, 1974), 202, distinguishes the *atra voluptas* denounced in the *Secretum* from the topos of the *voluptas dolendi* (pleasure of suffering), also highly documented in Petrarch (see, e.g., the "lugendi dulcedo" (sweetness of mourning) in *Fam.* 7.9.8), even though the two themes are connected. Rico also quotes a significant passage from *Sen.* 3.1.26: "ego vero malis meis pascor voluptate quadam effera, et qui fuerant gemitus cibi sunt, impletumque est in me seu Davidicum illud: 'Fuerunt michi lacrime mee panes die ac nocte,' sive illud Ovidianum: 'Cura dolorque animi lacrimeque cibi fuere'" (But I feed upon my misfortunes with a certain savage delight; my groans have become my sustenance. Fulfilled in me is either David's saying, 'My tears have become my bread day and night,' or Ovid's saying, 'Worry, tears, heartache—these have been my food'). In *Res seniles*, 1:185; *Letters of Old Age*, 1:77. Here, as often elsewhere in Petrarch, scriptural (Ps. 41.4 (42.4)) and classical references (Ovid, *Metamorphoses*, 10.75) go hand in hand.

8. Job 17.13: "in tenebris stravi lectulum meum" (I spread my couch in darkness).

9. Ps. 12.4 (13.3): "Inlumina oculos meos, ne umquam obdormiam in morte" (Give light to my eyes, or I will sleep the sleep of death); Job 33.28: "Liberavit animam suam ne pergeret in interitum" (He has redeemed my soul from going down to the Pit); Prv. 24.11: "Erue eos qui ducuntur ad mortem et qui trahuntur ad interitum liberare ne cesses" (If you hold back from rescuing those taken away to death, those who go staggering to the slaughter).

10. *Dvs.*1.8: "Nec quid agam scio" (I don't know what to do); *Secretum*: "Quid igitur faciam?" (What then shall I do?). The Latin text of *Dvs.* is from Martellotti, *De vita solitaria*, 96. Fenzi, *Secretum*, 230.

11. According to Coppini, the reference to the poet's youth here is evidence for backdating the psalms to a period prior to 1348, which is the date generally assigned to Petrarch's psalms. See Coppini, *Psalmi penitentiales*, 12.

12. The "signature themes" of shipwreck, fear of the sea, and sea storms are central to Petrarch's poetics. The maritime imagery is primarily used, as Theodore Cachey has cogently argued, to reveal Petrarch's deep "anxieties about his place or lack of it in the world," but it also conveys the aspiration "for some provisional home or stable dwelling in the world." Theodore J. Cachey, "From Shipwreck to Port: *Rvf* 189 and the Making of the *Canzoniere*," *MLN* 120 (2005): 30–49, at 33, 35. In the *Secretum* Petrarch writes, "Et ego, in mari magno sevoque ac turbido iactatus, tremulam cimbam fatiscentemque et rimosam ventis obluctantibus per

tumidos fluctus ago" (Tossed on a vast, wild, turbulent sea, I too steer my leaky, shattered, shuddering little boat through swollen waves in the face of the battling winds). Fenzi, *Secretum*, 132–34 (see also 299–300 n. 49 and 312 n. 126 for further references on this topic). The English translation of the *Secretum* is from *My Secret Book*, trans. and ed. Nicholas Mann (Cambridge, MA: Harvard University Press, 2016), 52–55; *Ep. metr.*, 1.14.34–39: "Sic, velut in dubiis deprensus nauta procellis, / cum ferus ante oculos socias absorbuit alnos / Neptunus, fragilem qui utero crepuisse carinam / sentit et illisos scopulis configere remos / ac procul horribiles clavum videt ire per undas, / hereo consilii incertus certusque pericli" (It is as if a sailor, seized by dangerous storms, and before whose eyes fierce Neptune devoured the ships of friends, now hears a cracking sound in the belly of his own brittle craft, sees the oars shattering, dashed against the rocks, and how his rudder is already drifting away in terrible waves. . . . I am stuck uncertain of what to do and certain of my danger); 118–20: "Vixisti in pelago nimis irrequietus iniquo" (You have lived your life far too restlessly on a hostile sea). See in particular *Rvf.* 26.2; 80; 151.1–2; 189; 235.5; 366.69–70. On this topic, see also Cachey, "*Peregrinus* (quasi) ubique"; Timothy Kircher's chapter, "The Sea as an Image of Temporality," in *The Poet's Wisdom: The Humanists, The Church, and the Formation of Philosophy in the Early Renaissance* (Leiden: Brill, 2006), 185–228; Michelangelo Picone, "Il motivo della 'navigatio' nel Canzoniere del Petrarca," *Atti e Memorie della Accademia Petrarca di Lettere, Arti e Scienze* 51 (1989): 291–307; Giuseppe Antonio Camerino, "'Per aspro mare': In margine a R.V.F. CLXXXIX," *Italianistica* 21.2–3 (1992): 503–9; Ps. 68.3 (69.2): "veni in profundum aquarum et flumen operuit me" (I have come into deep waters, and the flood sweeps over me).

13. The pursuit of a safe haven against the storms of life is another major theme, closely linked to that of the sea, sea storms, and shipwreck in Petrarch. As Cachey has observed, the space of writing is ultimately the quiet port where Petrarch not only is able to narrate, or better yet, navigate, the storms of life, but he is also able to dispel the threats of real ones. See Cachey's "*Peregrinus* (quasi) ubique," 381. The recourse to the port image in Petrarch also reveals strong echoes of the port metaphor present in the monastic tradition, where it is seen as the safe haven against the storms of life and prefiguration of the eschatological arrival at port. Worth noting, in this perspective, is the contraposition between a safe arrival at port and being tossed in the storms of life that emerges most vividly in Petrarch's letters when he refers to, or addresses, his Carthusian brother, Gherardo. See, e.g., *Fam.* 10.2.6: "Ceterum hic nunc animi labor et vehemens non magis meorum quam mundi malorum recordatio ante oculos michi constituit Gerardum cartusiensem monachum, germanum meum unicum virumque, me iudice, felicis-

simum et has omnes, quibus assidue quatimur, miserias supergressum, michi quoque sempiternum improperium, qui me in fluctibus laborante portum teneat et humanas ab alto despiciat tempestates" (This mental toil and vivid recollection of misfortunes, which are no greater for me than for the world, however, have brought before my eyes the image of Gherardo, my only brother and a Carthusian monk, in my opinion the happiest of men. Having overcome all these miseries with which we are constantly agitated, he has become for me a source of perennial reproach as he holds fast to his port, watching me labor in these waters, and disdains from his lofty perch human tempests); *Fam.* 10.3.5: "rudis nauta primo ventorum murmure terretur, gubernator antiquus qui totiens fatiscentem et exarmatam puppim perduxit in portum, ex alto despicit iratum mare. Spero autem in Illo qui te ab utero matris tue ad hoc laboriosum certe sed gloriosum iter assumpsit, ut per varias difficultates tutus in patriam pervenires, quod nulla te amplius rerum facies movebit, non 'luctus' non 'cure' non 'morbi' non 'senectus' non 'metus' non 'fames' non 'egestas'" (The new sailor is horrified by the first murmur of the winds, but the experienced helmsman who has so often led his battered and disarmed ship into port looks down haughtily at the stormy waters. I trust in Him who from your mother's womb has taken you on this journey, which is certainly laborious but also glorious, so that through various difficulties you could safely reach your homeland. Nothing can disturb you any longer: mourning or cares, illness or old age, fear or hunger or poverty); and *Fam.* 17.1.4: "te quoque nunc, frater, aspiciendo et miserando doctum ex indocto et de naufrago salvum fecit" (Now, my dear brother, watching over you and having compassion for you, He has transformed you from an unlearned to a learned man, from a shipwrecked to a rescued soul). *Le familiari*, 2:285, 287, and 3:222; and *Letters on Familiar Matters*, 2:56, 57–58, and 3:1, respectively.

14. See Petrarch's *Eclogue* 11.53: "levo . . . calle" (look to your left); *Fam.*, 12.3.6–7 and 7.17.1–2, 10–11, which provide a wealth of scriptural and classical citations; *Secretum*: "Cum enim recto tramite ascendens ad bivium pervenissem modestus et sobrius, et dextram iuberer arripere, ad levam—incautus dicam an contumax?—deflexi" (When I arrived at the crossroads by the straight path, modestly and soberly, and was ordered to turn to the right, I turned—should I say carelessly or culpably?—to the left). Fenzi, *Secretum*, 220; Mann, *My Secret Book*, 170–73. *Dvs.* 1.8: "Quam delectat illesum transisse pestifera et in bivio, ubi ad levam mors erat, dextrorsum tenuisse, eoque magis quo in partem alteram deliberatio pronior fuit!" (What a joy to have overcome all dangerous situations unscathed, and at the crossroads, where on the left was death, to have kept to the right—and all the more so, since the will inclined in the other direction); Martellotti, *De vita solitaria*, 96. The classical topos of the Pythagorean Y, representing

the *bivium* or proverbial fork in the road, soon Christianized by Lactantius (*Div. Inst.*, 6.3 and 4), is frequently mentioned by Petrarch; for the wealth of references, see Rico, *Vida u obra de Petrarca*, 304–11; Fenzi, *Secretum*, 369–70 n. 98. See also Bortolo Martinelli, *Il* Secretum *conteso* (Naples: Loffredo, 1982), 171–73; and Carlo Santini, "Nuovi accertamenti sull'ipotesi di raffronto tra Silvio e Petrarca," in *Preveggenze umanistiche di Petrarca* (Pisa: ETS, 1993), 111–39, 132–35.

15. *Fam.* 2.4.4: "et tenuiter video" (I discern only vaguely). *Le familiari*, 1:74; *Letters on Familiar Matters*, 1:79.

16. **Duellum** here recalls the same inner discord afflicting Franciscus in the *Secretum*. See Fenzi, *Secretum*, 138–40; Mann, *My Secret Book*, 62–63. See Giulio Goletti, "'Volentes unum aliud agimus': La questione del dissidio interiore e il cristianesimo petrarchesco," *Quaderni petrarcheschi* 7 (1990): 65–108. *Rvf.* 264.111–12: "l'aspra guerra / che 'ncontra me medesmo seppi ordire" (to suffer the bitter war that I have managed to combine against myself). Durling, *Petrarch's Lyric Poems*, 432–33.

17. Augustine, *Enarrationes in Psalmos*, 122.3: "Tu ipse irasceris peccatis tuis" (You will be angry with your sins); and *Confessions* 1.5: "irascaris mihi et mineris ingentes miserias" (you are angry with me and threaten me with great miseries). The Latin texts of Augustine are available at CC; the English translation of the *Enarrationes* is from *Expositions of the Psalms 121–150*, in *The Works of Saint Augustine: A Translation for the 21st Century*, ed. Edmund Hill, John E. Rotelle, and Allan D. Fitzgerald (Brooklyn, NY: New City Press, 1990), III/20:32. See *The Confessions*, ed. John E. Rotelle, trans. and introd. Maria Boulding (Hyde Park, NY: New City Press, 1997). Ps. 4.5: "Irascimini et nolite peccare" (When you are angry do not sin).

18. *Secretum*: "Quotiens enim, convalescendi avidus atque huius consilii non ignarus, fugam retentavi!" (How often when I wanted to recover have I tried to run away, in full awareness of this remedy). Fenzi, *Secretum*, 232; Mann, *My Secret Book*, 188–89.

19. *Rvf.* 81.1: "fascio antico" (ancient bundle); 62.10: "dispietato giogo" (pitiless yoke); 128.117: "l'usanza pessima et antica" (vicious and old customs); 270.1: "giogo anticho" (the old yoke); Durling, *Petrarch's Lyric Poems*, 184, 140, 442. *Secretum*: "vetustum servitutis iugum" (the ancient yoke of servitude); Fenzi, *Secretum*, 134; Mann, *My Secret Book*, 54–55. *Fam.*, 5.18.3: "durum inveterate consuetudinis iugum" (unyielding yoke of inveterate habit); *Le familiari*, 2:42; *Letters on Familiar Matters*, 1:276. All examples are counter to Christ's "suave iugum" (Mt. 11.30), which in Petrarch's courtly love poetry becomes "dolce giogo" (a sweet yoke) in *Rvf.* 197.3 and "dolce peso" (sweet weight) in *Rvf.* 205.2; Durling, *Petrarch's Lyric Poems*, 342, 350. See also *Dvs.* 2, where Petrarch cites Lam.

3.27 (the yoke of youth). Martellotti, *De vita solitaria*, 142. In Gal. 5.1, Paul warns against the "iugum servitutis" (yoke of slavery).

20. *Rvf.* 96.9–10: "Allor errai quando l'antica strada / di libertà mi fu precisa et tolta" (I went wrong when first my former path was cut off and blocked to me). Durling, *Petrarch's Lyric Poems*, 198. Central to *Dor.* is the invitation to be free ("Vacate" [Be still]) from Ps. 45.11 (46.10): "Vacate autem a supervacuis laboribus, qui corpus et spiritum fatigant, a concupiscentia carnis ac libidine, que totum fedant enervantque hominem, a concupiscentia oculorum, que obtentu scientie seducit, ab ambitione seculi, que uncis atque compedibus alligat, ab inutilis curis, que cor urunt facibus abditis, denique a peccatis omnibus, que infelicem animam torquent opprimuntque et interimunt" (Enjoy leisure from these superfluous tasks which wear out our body and spirit, from the carnal desires which defile and weaken our whole person, from the visual lusts which deflect us from the acquisition of knowledge, from the ambitions of this age, which ensnare us with their claws and shackles, from useless concerns which inflame our heart with unseen torches, and finally from all sins which torture, oppress, and destroy our unhappy soul). The Latin text of *Dor.* is from *De otio religioso*, ed. Giulio Goletti (Florence: Le Lettere, 2006), 34; the English translation is from Schearer, *On Religious Leisure*, 14. A central theme throughout Petrarch's psalms is the loss of spiritual freedom. See also *Rvf.* 97.1; 76.6–8.

21. See *Rvf.* 62.7–8: "sí ch' avendo le reti indarno tese, / il mio duro avversario" (so that, having spread his nets in vain, my harsh adversary); Durling, *Petrarch's Lyric Poems*, 140–41. *Ep. metr.* 1.14.125: "inter tot laqueos" (among the many snares); *Eclogue* 9.86: "quocunque movemur, / Mille parat medio laqueos et retia calle" ([death] sets his snares and his nets, wheresoever we turn in our panic); *Petrarch's Bucolicum Carmen*, 136–37. *Africa* 5.403–4: "Precipue tamen hec nitide suspecta iuvente / Pestis, etati pretendit retia nostre" (Youth in its early blossom / is subject to this evil, quick to spread / its nets to trap our unsuspecting years). The Latin text of the *Africa* is from *L'Africa: Edizione critica per cura di Nicola Festa; corredata di un ritratto e cinque tavole fuori testo* (Florence: Sansoni, 1926), 117. The English translation is from *Petrarch's Africa*, trans. and annotated Thomas Bergin and Alice Wilson (New Haven, CT: Yale University Press, 1977), 97; Ps. 56.7 (57.6): "rete paraverunt gressibus meis" (They set a net for my steps); Ps. 123.7 (124.7): "Anima nostra quasi avis erepta est de laqueo venantium laqueus contritus est et nos liberati sumus" (We have escaped like a bird from the snare of the hunters; the snare is broken, and we have escaped); Ps. 118.61 (119.61): "Funes impiorum inplicaverunt me" (Though the cords of the wicked ensnare me); Prv. 5.22: "Iniquitates suae capiunt impium et funibus peccatorum suorum constringitur" (The iniquities of the wicked ensnare them, and they are caught in the

coils of their sin). References to snares, traps, and nets in Petrarch are numerous; see, e.g., *Rvf.* 55.15: "tende lacci" ([Love] puts out snares); 59.4: "nascose il laccio" ([Love] hid the noose); 89.10: "il giogo et le catene e i ceppi" (the yoke and the chains and the shackles); 96.4: "ogni laccio" (every noose); 106.5: "un laccio . . . tese fra l'erba" (a . . . snare . . . stretched in the grass); 181.1: "una leggiadra rete" (a gay net); Durling, *Petrarch's Lyric Poems*, 132–33, 136–37, 192–93, 198–99, 214–15, 326–27. See also *Ep. metr.* 1.6.44. On this topic in Petrarch and Augustine, see Evelyine Luciani, *Les Confessions de Saint Augustin dans les lettres de Petrarque* (Paris: Études Augustiniennes, 1982), 42. Although snares and chains pertain to the spiritual-religious imagery, their metaphorical use figures prominently in the erotic-courtly poetic tradition as well. On this topic, see in particular Rico, *Vida u obra de Petrarca*, 251.

22. See *Dor.*: "inter tot invia, tot prerupta, tot lubrica, tot latronum insidias" (amidst so many dead ends, so many steep and ragged climbs, so many slippery places, amidst so many ambushes by bandits); Goletti, *De otio religioso*, 230; Schearer, *On Religious Leisure*, 131.

23. *Fam.* 2.9.14: "presertim si adolescentie sue meminit, quam vagam et aberrantem miseratus Omnipotens retraxit ad rectum iter" (especially if he recalls his own youth which the merciful Almighty brought back to the straight path from its wanderings and deviations); *Le familiari*, 1:93; *Letters on Familiar Matters*, 1:101.

24. Ps. 36.13 (37.13): "Dominus deridebit eum [impius]" (but the Lord laughs at the wicked), also cited in *Sen.* 1.7.30; Ps. 2.4: "habitator caeli ridebit Dominus" (He who sits in the heavens laughs).

25. *Eclogue* 8.74: "tenuit me pestifer usus" (The strength of a vicious habit held me); *Fam.* 5.18.3: "invaluit in me durum inveterate consuetudinis iugum" (the unyielding yoke of an inveterate habit prevailed over me); *Fam.* 10.3.26: "visco consuetudinis pessime delinitus" (besmeared with the lime of an awful habit); *Le familiari*, 2:42, 292; *Letters on Familiar Matters*, 1:276; 2:62. In Augustine's *Confessions* 6.12.22: "consuetudo satiandae insatiabilis concupiscentiae me captum excruciabat" (the habit of trying to satisfy that insatiable desire tortured me and held me captive); 8.5.12: "Lex enim peccati est violentia consuetudinis" (For the law of sin is the violence of custom). See Luciani, *Les Confessions*, 82–83, 128–29. On postponing one's conversion, see Fenzi, *Secretum*, 172; Mann, *My Secret Book*, 106–7. See also the references to Augustine's *Confessions* in Rico, *Vida u obra de Petrarca*, 191; *Dor.*: "Gravi enim sarcina premimur dum vivimus, imo vero dum viviere dicimur; dum hic sumus mutatique decor animisepe veteribus maculis clam repente respergitur, et adolescentie probra sensim longe consuetudinis obducto velamine rursus ita se ingerunt et iam fessam atque emeritam senectutem

insequuntur" (We suffer a heavy burden while we are here, while the comeliness of our renewed soul is often suddenly and secretly splattered with old stains, and while the disgraces of youth, enveloped by the mantle of long habit, ingrain themselves again in us and pursue us in our tired and exhausted old age); Goletti, *De otio religioso*, 179–80; Schearer, *On Religious Leisure*, 100. *Ep. metr.* 1.6.130–31: "reposcens / mancipium secura suum" (imperiously demands the slave back). In *Rvf.*, see 80.36: "l'usata vita" (my accustomed life) and 211.2: "usanza mi trasporta" (Habit carries me away); Durling, *Petrarch's Lyric Poems*, 182–83.

26. Following Cochin's edition, which mistakenly replaces "inicit" with "vincit," in Gigliucci's version the sentence reads: "and ties his pointlessly rebellious hands." On Cochin's edition, see Coppini, *Psalmi penitentiales*, 18–19.

27. Ps. 50.3 (51.2): "Miserere mei Deus secundum magnam misericordiam tuam" (Have mercy on me, O God, according to your abundant mercy); Ps. 56.2 (57.1): "Miserere mei Deus miserere mei" (Be merciful to me, O God; be merciful to me). See Augustine's *Confessions* 10.4.5; 12.27.37. See also *Rvf.* 62.12; 366.120.

28. *Ep. metr.* 1.14.122–23: "Quis me de faucibus hostis / eripiat?" (Who can rescue me from the jaws of the enemy?). See also 1.6.152–55; *Secretum*: "Miserere, Iesu, fer opem: 'eripe me his, invicte, malis,'" (Have pity on me, Jesus, help me: 'Pluck me, o invincible one, from these misfortunes') where Petrarch cites *Aeneid* 6.365; Fenzi, *Secretum*, 130; Mann, *My Secret Book*, 48–51. The same quotation is in *Dor.*; see Goletti, *De otio religioso*, 172–73; Schearer, *On Religious Leisure*, 87. See *Fam.* 2.9.17; 23.12.20. See also Fenzi, *Secretum*, 309 n. 108; and Rico, *Vida u obra de Petrarca*, 100. Finally, Petrarch provides a series of scriptural citations on divine mercy in *Dvs.* 1.4; Martellotti, *De vita solitaria*, 54–57.

PSALM II

29. Ps. 24.2 (25.2): "ne confundar" (do not let me be put to shame).

30. On Christ's power to resurrect the dead, see Mk. 5.21–43; Lk. 7.11–17; Jn. 11.1–44; Mt. 11.5: "Mortui resurgunt" (the dead are raised). See also Ez. 37.12–13: "Ecce ego aperiam tumulos vestros et educam vos de sepulchris vestris . . . et scietis quia ego Dominus, cum aperuero sepulchra vestra et eduxero vos de tumulis vestris populus meus" (I am going to open your graves and bring you up from your graves . . . and you shall know that I am the Lord when I open your graves and bring you up from your graves, O my people). Cold and ice are images that recur frequently in *Rvf.*; see 264.127: "ò il cor via più freddo—de la paura che gelata neve" (and my heart is much colder with fear than frozen snow);

68.10: "M'agghiaccio dentro" (turn to ice within); Durling, *Petrarch's Lyric Poems*, 433, 149.

31. Ecclesiasticus 5.5: "neque adicias peccatum super peccatum" (do not add sin to sin).

32. Aquinas (?), *Adora te devote*, vv. 23–25: "me immundum munda tuo sanguine / cuius una stilla salvum facere / totum mundum posset omni scelere" (cleanse me, who am unclean, in your blood / One drop of which would be enough to save the whole world of all its defilement). *Fam.* 10.5.27: "scelerum meorum sordes" (the base ugliness of my sins); *Le familiari*, 2:317; *Letters on Familiar Matters*, 2:81.

33. *Rvf.* 23.25: "adamantino smalto" (an adamantine hardness); 39.8: "freddo smalto" (cold stone); 366.111–12. Durling, 60–61, 104–5. Rico, in *Vida u obra de Petrarca*, 65, sees a parallel here for the image of the waters originating from the symbolic stone of the soul with Petrarch's *Oratio quotidiana* (Tibi, Domine Ihesu Christe, of June 1, 1335): "Tange lapidem cordis mei, unde exeant fontes lacrimarum quibus abluantur peccatorum meorum vulnera" (touch the stone of my heart, from which founts of tears may emerge to cleanse the wounds of my sins). See "Petrarch's Prayers" in this volume. And see M. Léopold Delisle, "Notice sur un livre annoté par Pétrarque (ms. latin 2201 de la Bibliothèque Nationale)," in *Notices et extraits des manuscrits de la Bibliothèque Nationale et autres bibliothèques*, tome 35, parte II (Paris: Klincksieck, 1897), 393–408, at 397. Ps. 113.8 (114.8): "qui convertit petram in paludes aquarum silicem in fontes aquarum" (who turns the rock into a pool of water, the flint into a spring of water). See also Vincenzo Fera's perceptive reading of these verses in "Testo e gestualità: Un versetto penitenziale del Petrarca," *Quaderni Veneti* 2 (2013): 119–28.

34. 2 Pet. 2.22: "et sus lota in volutabro luti" (The sow is washed only to wallow in the mud); Ps. 79.14 (80.13): "vastavit eam aper de silva et omnes bestiae agri depastae est eam" (The boar from the forest ravages it [the Lord's vine], and all that move in the field feed on it). On the image of the boar, see Pozzi, "Petrarca, i Padri e e soprattutto la Bibbia," 152–53. Apparently, Petrarch aspires to change from pig (who dwells in mud and swamps) to deer (who in Ps. 42.1 "Desiderat ad fontes aquarium" (longs for flowing streams); this contrast is reiterated in scripture and patristic literature; see, e.g., Sedulius, *Collectaneum miscellaneum* 70.8: "Aper in palude, cervus ad fontes currit" (The boar in the marsh, the deer running to the springs); in *Sedulii Scotti collectaneum miscellaneum*, ed. Dean Simpson (Turnhout: Brepols, 1988), 286. See also Ambrose, *Hexaemeron*, Liber Tertius, De Opere Tertii Diei, 33, Caput I, Sermo 4.2.4. The Latin text is available at CC, https://www.mlat.uzh.ch/browser?path=958&text=6958.

35. A fascinating expression suggesting that God can take pleasure in the soul of a sinner through forgiveness whereas the sinner hates himself in remembering his fault.

36. Ps. 29.6 (30.5): "Ad vesperum commorabitur fletus et in matutino laus" (Weeping may linger for the night, but joy comes with the morning).

37. *Fam.* 9.1.1: "Solebant leta tristibus, amaris dulcia miscere; nunc, heu, tristia et amara omnia" (Once they mingled joy with sorrow, sweetness with bitterness,; now, alas, all things are sad and bitter); *Fam.* 20.8.2: "sic amara dulcibus, leta tristibus, obscuris clara, dubiis certa permisces" (you shall mix the bitter with the sweet, the happy with the sad, the bright with the dark, the certain with the doubtful); *Fam.* 23.12.34: "miscentur leta tristibus, clara obscuris, tranquilla turbidis, adversa felicibus, et in magno acervo rerum humanarum, si ad cribrum veniat, boni minimum, mali plurimum deprehendetur" (Happiness alternates with sadness, light with dark, peace with turmoil, fortune with misfortune, while a close examination of most human affairs would reveal a minimum of good and maximum of evil); *Le familiari*, 2:211; 4:27, 193; *Letters on Familiar Matters*, 2:1; 3:144, 287, respectively. As Gigliucci notes, the combination of opposites here tends to a sense of balance. Elsewhere instead, Petrarch's oxymoronic combination points more to an almost tragic contradictory laceration of subject and object. See Roberto Gigliucci, *Oxymoron Amoris* (Anzio: De Rubeis, 1990), 53–61.

38. *De sui ipsius et multorum ignorantia* 2.27: "de me diffidentia, de te spes" (Let me have diffidence in myself, and hope in You, O Lord). Marsh, *Invectives*, 246–47.

39. *Rvf.* 234.1, 5: "O cameretta . . . O letticciuol" (O little room . . . O little bed); 216.1–4: "la notte . . . trovomi in pianto" (at night . . . I find that I am in tears); 226.8: "duro campo di battaglia il letto" (my bed is a harsh battlefield); Durling, *Petrarch's Lyric Poems*, 392–93, 372–73, 382–83, respectively. Ps. 6.7: "Laboravi in gemitu meo, lavabo per singulas noctes lectum meum, in lacrimis meis stratum meum rigabo" (I am weary with my moaning; every night I flood my bed with tears; I drench my couch with my weeping); Job 33.19: "Increpat quoque per dolorem in lectulo." A bed flooded with tears is in stark contrast to the "lectulus floridus" (Our couch is green) of the Song of Songs 1.15; but see 3.1. Also worth noting is the "lectulus vite" in *Fam.* 15.4.15: "sed non ideo mollis aut equus lectulus meus erit—lectulus vite huius in quo fessus iaceo—, quin potius asper inamenus immundus iniquus scrupulosus et qui sanissimos etiam vehementer exagitet" (but my bed will not for all that be softer or unrumpled—the bed of this life on which I lie exhausted—but rather rough, unpleasant, soiled, uneven, lumpy such as would torture even the most healthy body); *Le familiari*, 3:317; *Letters on*

30 *Petrarch's Penitential Psalms and Prayers*

Familiar Matters, 2:260. It is worth noting that this particular verse is cited by Petrarch in his letter of 1371 to Francesco Bruni when referring to his *devotiuncula*; see Pancheri, *Lettere disperse*, 488.

40. *Fam.* 19.16.11: "Spes prima et ultima Cristus est" (Christ is the first and last hope). The verse recalls Sedulius, *Carmen paschale*, 1.60: "Omnipotens aeterne Deus, spes unica mundi"; see Giuseppe Velli, "Petrarca e i poeti cristiani," *Studi petrarcheschi* 6 (1989): 171–78, at 177.

PSALM III

41. The final image recalls Ps. 68.3 (69.2): "Infixus sum in limo profundi / et non possum consistere" (I sink in deep mire, where there is no foothold); and Ps. 106.26 (107.26): "anima eorum in adflictiones consumitur" (their courage melted away in their calamity). See also Augustine's *Confessions* 3.11.20: "in illo limo profundi . . . volutatus sum" (I wallowed in the mud of that deep pit); Ovid, *Ex Ponto* 4.2.19: "pectora sic mea sunt limo vitiata malorum" (so my mind has been injured by the silt of misfortune); Arthur Leslie Wheeler, *Ovid with an English Translation: Tristia, Ex Ponto*, vol. 10 (Cambridge, MA: Harvard University Press, 1965), 428; *Secretum*: "ipsi te ceno subruant" (drag you down into the mud); Fenzi, *Secretum*, 256; Mann, *My Secret Book*, 220–21. *Fam.* 4.12.29: "quasi ad nichil aliud nati simus, quam ut, inter mundi fluctus et ludibria fortune perpetuo turbine iactandi, carnis nostre tenacissimo limo ac sordibus hereamus" (as if we were born for no other reason than to cling to the thick filth and to the dregs of our flesh, wallowing in the eternal whirling of the world's vicissitudes and the mockery of fortune); *Le familiari*, 1:183; *Letters on Familiar Matters*, 1:207. *Ep. metr.* 2.3.59–60: "ignaros quo nostra tamen corpuscula limo subsistant" (and yet they do not know what clay our bodies are made of); Schönberger, *Epistulae Metricae*, 124.

42. Ps. 101.4, 12 (102.3, 11): "quoniam consumpti sunt sicut fumus dies mei . . . dies mei quasi umbra inclinati sunt" (For my days pass away like smoke. . . . My days are like a lengthening shadow); Ps. 77.33 (78.33): "et consumpsit in vanitate dies eorum et annos eorum cum velociter" (So he made their days vanish like a breath and their years in terror). Job 9.25: "dies mei velociores fuerunt cursore fugerunt et non viderunt bonum" (My days are swifter than a runner; they flee away; they see no good).

43. Ps. 12.2 (13.2): "usquequo ponam consilia in anima mea" (How long must I bear pain); *Fam.* 10.1.3: "Quid enim . . . , quasi venturi certus, tempus in consiliis expendis?" (Why, then . . . do you spend so much time in deliberations as if certain of the future?); *Fam.* 23.2.15: "Ecce nun Caesar . . . in consiliis vitam

teris" (And so, O Caesar . . . you are wasting your life in deliberations). *Le familiari*, 2:278 and 4:161; *Letters on Familiar Matters*, 2:278 and 2:259, respectively. On the central theme of time's fleeting nature, see *Rvf.* 272.1: "La vita fugge et non s'arresta una hora" (Life flees and does not stop an hour); 128.97–99: "Signor', mirate come 'l tempo vola / et sí come la vita / fugge, et la morte n'è sovra le spalle" (Lords: see how time flies and how life flees, and how Death is at our backs); Durling, *Petrarch's Lyric Poems*, 450–51 and 262–63, respectively; *Africa* 2.347–50: "Facili labuntur secula passu: / tempora diffugiunt; ad mortem curritis" (The centuries easily slip away: the times flee away; to death you hasten); *De remediis* 1.1 (where Petrarch cites Cicero's *Tusculanus*, 1.31.76: "volat enim aetas" [time indeed flies], evoked also in *Fam.* 1.3.2, along with Augustine's *De civitate dei* 13.10). See in particular *Fam.* 24.1 (providing a wealth of citations from various *auctoritates*: Horace, Juvenal, Virgil, Ovid, Seneca, Cicero), as well as 21.12.

44. Job 17.1: "spiritus meus adtenuabitur dies mei breviabuntur et solum mihi superest sepulchrum" (My spirit is broken; my days are extinct; the grave is ready for me). *Secretum*: "non potestis oculos advertere, ubi non eis occurrat proprie mortalitatis effigies" (there is nowhere you can look without being struck by the image of your own mortality), where, however, the reflection on one's own mortality has beneficial and salvific value; Fenzi, *Secretum*, 122; Mann, *My Secret Book*, 40–41. On this topic, see Rico and Fenzi but also Martinelli, *Il "Secretum" conteso* (Naples: Loffredo, 1982), 177; and Gigliucci, *Lo spettacolo della morte* (Anzio: De Rubeis, 1944), 155–65. In *Dor.* it is a serious mistake to disregard the contemplation of death: "Illa maior periculosiorque dementia, quod nec conditione nature nec tot assidue exemplis inducimur ut de morte cogitemus, non credo quia prorsus mortalitatis et imbecillitatis obliti simus, sed iuvat oculos avertere ne venientem videamus, quasi non sit tutius adventantem hostem prospicere, quam conniventibus oculis expectare dum feriat" (There is one greater and more dangerous madness: neither our nature nor so many constant examples persuade us to think about death. I do not believe that we have totally forgotten our mortality and weakness, but we prefer to avert our eyes so that we may not see it coming, as if it were safer not to see the enemy approaching. Therefore, we wait with eyes shut until he strikes); Goletti, *De otio religioso*, 164; Schearer, *On Religious Leisure*, 91.

45. Mt. 24.51, 25.30: "illic erit fletus et stridor dentium" (where there will be weeping and gnashing of teeth); see also 22.13 and Job 17.1: "solum mihi superest sepulchrum" (the grave is ready for me).

46. *Secretum*, citing Horace, *Odes* 4.7.17–18: "an addicant hodierne crastina vite / tempora dii superi?" (Who knows whether the gods above will add a

tomorrow to the life of this day?); Fenzi, *Secretum*, 266; Mann, *My Secret Book*, 234–34. See Mt. 6.34: "Nolite ergo esse solliciti in crastinum; crastinus enim dies sollicitus erit sibi ipse" (So do not worry about tomorrow, for tomorrow will bring worries of its own). See also *Dvs.* 1.8: "Nunquam pendere desinet, qui in crastinum pendebit" (The one who waits on the morrow will never stop waiting); Martellotti, *De vita solitaria*, 112; and Seneca, *Ad Lucilium Epistulae Morales* 1.2: "sic fiet ut minus ex crastino pendeas, si hodierno manum inieceris" (hold every hour in your grasp, and you will not need to depend so much upon tomorrow's); the Latin text is available at CC, https://www.mlat.uzh.ch/browser?path=12351 &text=12587. See also *Ep. metr.* 1.14.69: "crastina pertractans animo presentia perdes" (with only tomorrow on your mind, you lose the present hour); Schönberger, *Epistulae Metricae*, 106.

47. On a less anxious view of the inner storms, see *Fam.* 15.12.1: "inter animi mei fluctus et rerum scopulos" (amidst the billows of my mind and the reefs of my affairs). A more tormented description appears in the previous letter 15.11.3, to the same addressee, where Petrarch writes, "multis consiliis ceu fluctibus iactatus" (buffeted by countless considerations as if they were waves). *Fam.* 8.3.18: "pectoris mei fluctus" (the inlets of my heart); *Fam.* 5.1.3: "procellarum animi mei" (the storms of my mind); *Le familiari*, 3:165, 164; 2:4; *Letters on Familiar Matters*, 2:282; 1:400, 1:228. Seneca, *De iram*, 3.10.2: "procellarum animos vexantium" (the storms tormenting the souls); *De Tranquillitate*, 10.7: "animi fluctibus" (the waves of the mind); *Herc. fur.* 1092: "pelle insanos / fluctus animi" (drive the waves of madness from your spirit). Equally relevant in Petrarch is the topos of the agitated waves of life, of the world.

48. Ps.15.7 (16.7): "Benedicam Domino qui dedit consilium mihi" (I bless the Lord, who gives me counsel); Ps. 118.34, 125 (119.34, 125): "doce me" (Give me understanding).

49. Ps. 142.10 (143.10): "Doce me facere voluntatem tuam" (Teach me to do your will); *Fam.* 19.12.5: "fons actionum omnium voluntas deest" ([his] will, which is the fount of all deeds, is absent); *Le familiari*, 3:337; *Letters on Familiar Matters*, 3:101. The themes of lack of will or weakness with related *perplexitas* are central to Petrarch's introspective world; see *Fam.* 15.11.2: "Non plene igitur velle possum quod frustra me velle video; hinc michi labor et rerum infinita perplexitas" (Therefore I cannot fully want what I see myself wanting in vain, whence my distress and my infinite perplexity); *Le familiari*, 3:163–64; *Letters on Familiar Matters*, 2:281. See also the first pages of the first book of the *Secretum*, with the valuable commentaries of Rico, Fenzi, and Martinelli.

50. Ps. 17.18 (18.17): "liberavit me de inimicis meis potentissimis" (He delivered me from my strong enemy); Ps. 30.16 (31.15): "Libera me de manu inimi-

corum meorum" (deliver me from the hand of my enemies); Ps. 58.2 (59.2) and Ps. 142.9 (143.9): "Erue me de inimicis meis Deus meus" (Save me, O Lord, from my enemies). As is often the case in Petrarch, scriptural sources are interwoven with classical ones. See Virgil, *Aeneid* 6.365: "eripe me his, invicte, malis," often cited by Petrarch (*Fam.* 2.9.17; *Fam.* 23.12.19; *Secretum* (Fenzi, 130; Mann, 48–49).

51. Ps. 137.8 (138.8): "opera manuum tuarum ne dimittas" (Do not forsake the work of your hands).

52. Ps. 21.12 (22.11): "quoniam non est adiutor" (and there is no one to help); Ps. 106.12 (107.12): "et non erat qui adiuvaret" (with no one to help).

53. The suffering of the sinner is part of his conversion, as both Aquinas (and Augustine) seem to suggest: "Peccatum ad duo ordinatur: ad unum quidem per se, scilicet ad damnationem; ad aliud autem ex misericordis Dei providentia, scilicet ad sanationem, in quantum Deus permittit aliquos cadere in peccatum, ut peccatum suum agnoscentes, humilientur et convertantur, sicut Augustinus dicit in libro de Natura et Gratia (Cap. 27, 28)" (Now sin has a twofold relation—to one thing directly, viz., to the sinner's damnation—to another, by reason of God's mercy or providence, viz., that the sinner may be healed, insofar as God permits some to fall into sin, that by acknowledging their sin, they may be humbled and converted, as Augustine states (*De Nat. et Grat.* xxii)). In *Summa theologiae*, 1ᵃ 2ᵒᵉ quaest. 79 art. 4. The Latin text is available at CC, https://www.mlat.uzh.ch/browser?path=/11975; the English translation is at https://aquinas.cc/la/en/~ST.III.Q79.A4.CC.

54. "Sit mihi pars . . . tempus egestatis" resurfaces again in the the letter of 1371 to Francesco Bruni where Petrarch refers to his psalms as his *devotiuncula*; Pancheri, *Lettere disperse*, 488. See psalm 2 n. 11.

55. On the theme of the right and wrong path, see psalm 1 n. 54. Ps. 24.4 (25.4): "vias tuas Domine ostende mihi semitas tuas doce me" (Make me to know your ways, O Lord; teach me your paths); Ps. 26.11 (27.11): "ostende mihi Domine viam tuam et deduc me in semita recta propter insidiatores meos" (Teach me your way, O Lord, and lead me on a level path because of my enemies); Ps. 26.11 (27.11): "deduc me in semita recta" (and lead me on a level path); *Rvf.* 25.5: "Or ch'al dritto cammin l'ha Dio rivolta" (now that God has turned it back to the right path); Durling, *Petrarch's Lyric Poems*, 70–71.

56. Lk. 24.29: "quoniam advesperascit et inclinata est iam dies" (because it is almost evening, and the day is now nearly over).

57. *Secretum*: "advesperascit enim et nox est amica predonibus" (twilight is here, and the night favors brigands); Fenzi, *Secretum*, 240; Mann, *My Secret Book*, 200–201. *Fam.* 15.8.10: "tempus est ad vesperam subsistendi figendique anchoram, ne nox deprehendat errantes" (at vespers it is time to halt and cast anchor

lest the night overtake us in our wanderings); *Le familiari*, 3:155; *Letters on Familiar Matters*, 2:273.

58. Ps. 32.13 (33.13): "de caelo respexit Dominus vidit omnes filios Adam" (The Lord looks down from heaven; he sees all humankind).

Psalm IV

59. Ps. 43.16 (44.15): "ignominia faciei meae cooperuit me" (and shame has covered my face); see also Ps. 68.8 and 20 (69.7, 19). *Confusio* e *rubor*, are frequently linked in scripture: see Ps. 68.7 (69.6); Is. 45.16 and 54.4.

60. On "vicissitudines temporum," see Cicero, *De natura deorum* 1.20 and 36; Augustine, *Confessions*, 12.12; and *Fam.* 1.7.15: "Sunt mire varietates rerum ac vicissitudines temporum, quas occurrens natura fastidio vigilantissimo artificio meditata est" (Wonderful indeed are the variety of things and the changes of seasons which nature gladly planned to combat our boredom); *Le familiari*, 1:38; *Letters on Familiar Matters*, 1:39.

61. Ps. 73.16–17 (74.16–17): "Tua est dies et tua est nox tu ordinasti luminaria et solem tu statuisti omnes terminos terrae aestatem et hiemem tu plasmasti" (Yours is the day, yours also the night; you established the luminaries and the sun. You have fixed all the bounds of the earth; you made summer and winter); Ps. 103.19–20 (104.19–20): "Fecit lunam per tempora sol cognovit occubitum suum posuisti tenebras et facta est nox" (You have made the moon to mark the seasons; the sun knows its time for setting. You make darkness, and it is night). On the beauty of creation, the dignity of humans, and happiness in this life, see in particular *De remediis*, 2.93: "An autem, ut ex multis summam delibem, parva vobis gaudii causa est, imago illa et similitudo Dei creatoris, humana intus in anima? ingenium, memoria, providentia, eloquium, tot inventa, tot artes hinc animo famulantes, hinc corpori, quibus necessitates vestre omnes divino beneficio, comprehense sunt? tante quoque opportunitates, et tam varie rerum species, non necessitati tantum vestre, sed oblectationi servientium miris et ineffabilibus modis? tanta vis radicum, tot herbarum suci, tot florum tam iocunda varietas? tot odorum et colorum et saporum et sonorum ex contrariis orta concordia? tot animalia celo, terris ac pelago, non nisi vestris usibus dedita, hominisque solius ad obsequium creata? nisi enim peccati iugum sponte subiissetis, omnium que sub celo sunt dominium haberetis. Adde collium prospectus, apricationes vallium, umbrosos saltus, algentesque Alpes, et tepentia litora. Adde tot salubres scatebras aquarum, tot sulphureos fumantesque, tot nitidos ac gelidos fontes, tot infusa et circumfusa terris maria, tot amnes assidue mobiles, et immobili stabilitate certissimos regno-

rum fines. Adde lacus, maris emulos, et stagna iacentia, et rivos inter montium convexa precipites, et floreas ripas, riparumque thoros, et prata recentia rivis" (Now, considering essentials, is it so small a joy to know that there is the likeness of God the Creator depicted within the human soul, your mind, your memory, foresight, and speech; that so many inventions and arts are here to serve your soul and body, whose needs are all provided for by the good Lord; that great opportunities and desirable things are supplied in His marvelous and ineffable ways, not just for survival, but for your delight? So many efficacious roots and juices of herbs, the pleasant variety of so many flowers, the harmony by contraries of scents, colors, tastes and sounds; so many living creatures in the air, upon the land, and in the sea—all for your use, created to obey your wishes! Had you not, on your own accord, submitted to the yoke of sin, you would now govern all things under heaven. Add here the beckoning hills, the sun-drenched valleys and shady glens, the icy Alps, and the mild seashore, the wholesome bubbling waters and the springs, some sulfurous and steaming, some clear and cold—the sea upon the earth, the ever-changing streams, and the borders of kingdoms of never changing permanence. Add lakes as big as oceans, swamps, the waters rushing through mountain gorges and those flowering edges). The Latin text is from Christophe Carraud, *Pétrarque: Les remedes aux deux fortunes*, 2 vols. (Grenoble: Millon, 2002), 1:950. The English translation is from Rawski, *Petrarch's Remedies for Fortune Fair and Foul*, 3:224–25 and 4:360. *Fam.* 10.3.50–52. See also Pozzi, "Petrarca, i padri e soprattutto la Bibbia," 164–66.

62. Ps. 8.4 (8.3): "videbo enim caelos tuos opera digitorum tuorum" (When I look at your heavens, the work of your fingers).

63. *Fam.* 8.3.17: "tot lucidos fontes, tot vaga flumina, tot piscosos lacus" (so many shining springs, so many rambling rivers, so many lakes full of fish); *Le familiari*, 2:161; *Letters on Familiar Matters*, 1:400.

64. Ps. 8.7 (8.6): "dabis ei potestatem super opera manuum tuarum cuncta posuisti sub pedibus eius" (You have given them dominion over the works of your hands; you have put all things under their feet). On the following sentence, see *Fam.*10.3.51: "innumerabilium rerum vobis presidia et oblectationes et ornamenta congessi" (I who formed for you . . . the protection, the delights, and ornaments of countless things); *Le familiari*, 2:298; *Letters on Familiar Matters*, 2:66.

65. Petrarch seems to refer specifically to himself when acknowledging the many gifts God bestowed upon him even though the personal pronoun "me" appears only later (v. 18).

66. Ps. 8.6–7 (8.5): "Minues eum paulo minus a Deo gloria et decore coronabis eum" (Yet you have made them a little lower than God and crowned them with glory and honor).

67. Cicero, *De natura deorum*, 2.133: "Faciliusque intellegetur a dis immortalibus hominibus esse provisum, si erit tota hominis fabricatio perspecta omnisque humanae naturae figura atque perfectio" (That the immortal gods provided for humans will be more easily understood if we examine the whole structure of human beings, and every form and perfection of human nature). The Latin text is from *De natura deorum*, ed. Arthur Stanley Pease (Cambridge, MA: Harvard University Press, 1955), 896–97. On Cicero's *De natura deorum*, see *De sui ipsius*: "Denique corporum ac sensuum et membrorum compage ac dispositione mirabilia" (next, the marvelous construction and composition of our bodies, members, and senses); The Latin text and English translation are from Marsh, *Invectives*, 286–87.

68. Ovid, *Metamorphoses*, 1.85–86: "os homini sublime dedit caelumque videre / iussit et erectos ad sidera tollere vultus," (to man, the gods gave an upright countenance to survey the heavens, and to look upward to the stars) cited by Petrarch in a marginal note at the beginning of chapter 12 of Cassiodorus's *De anima*, in MS Paris Lat. 2201. See Delisle, "Notice sur un livre," 402; Cicero, *De natura deorum*, 2.140: "Qui [scil. dei] primum eos [scil. homines] humo excitatos celsos et erectos constituit, ut deorum cognitionem caelum intuentes capere possent" (In the first place they [the gods] made them [humans] tall and upright, raised aloft from the ground, that they might be able, through their gaze being turned upon the sky, to obtain a knowledge of the divine existence); *De remediis*, 2.93. On the human body in patristic literature see, among others, Ambrose, *Hexaemeron* 6.9.54; Cassiodorus, *De anima*, 11; Lactantius, *De opificio dei*, 7.

69. Cicero, *De natura deorum*, 2.132: "artes denique innumerabiles ad victum et ad vitam necessariae" (and finally the innumerable arts necessary for subsistence and life); *Eclogue* 1.99–100: "quibus addidit artes / innumeras" (and to each He has added / arts beyond number); *Petrarch's Bucolicum Carmen*, 12–13.

70. "Scis quid ille tibi suggerit, quas vias et que devia, quid sequendum vitandum ve pronuntiet" (You know what it is suggesting, which roads are right, and which wrong, and it will tell you what to follow or to avoid); Fenzi, *Secretum*, 280; Mann, *My Secret Book*, 252–53. *Fam.* 2.9.13: "quid sequendum declinandum ve sit docens" (teaching him what is to be pursued and what is to be avoided); *Le familiari*, 1:93; *Letters on Familiar Matters*, 1:100–101; *Oratio quotidiana*: "Dirige gressus meos in viam pacis et per semitam mandatorum tuorum a quibus tam longe aberravi" (guide my steps on the way to peace and on the paths of your commandments, from which I have strayed so far away). See "Latin Prayers" in this volume. See also the *brevior* version, *Salus mea Christe Ihesu*, of July 10, 1338: "gressus meos dirige in viam salutis eterne" (guide my steps on the way to eternal

salvation). See Marco Santagata, *Per le moderne carte* (Bologna: Il Mulino, 1990), 172 n. 29; *Dor.*: "Habemus quo vite cursum dirigamus" (We have where to direct the course of life); Goletti, *De otio religioso*, 250–51; Ps. 15.11 (16.11): "Notas mihi fecisti vias vitae" (You show me the path of life); Ps. 39.3 (40.2): "stabilivit gressus meos" (making my steps secure); Ps. 118.133 (119.133): "gressus meos firma" (Keep my steps steady); Ps. 142.8 (143.8): "Notam fac mihi viam" (Teach me the way I should go).

71. Ps. 26.5 (27.5): "Abscondit enim me in umbra sua in die pessima abscondet me in secreto tabernaculi sui" (he will conceal me under the cover of his tent; he will set me high on a rock).

72. Augustine, *Sermo* 235.2: "in via cum illis tamquam comes ambulabat, et ipse dux erat" (He was walking with them along the the road like a companion and was himself the leader). The sermon is on the Emmaus episode (Lk. 24.13–35), clearly present in Petrarch's psalms. The English translation is from Augustine, *Sermons 230–272B*, in *The Works of Saint Augustine: A Translation for the 21st Century* (New Rochelle: New City Press, 1990), III/7:41.

73. Job 34.21: "et dilataverunt super me os suum dixerunt va va vidit oculus noster" (For his eyes are upon the ways of mortals, and he sees all their steps).

74. *Oratio quotidiana*: "cadentem substenta, iacentem erige" (support me, for I fall; lift me up, for I am prostrate). See "Petrarch's Prayers" in this volume.

75. *Dor.* 2.16: "Esto igitur ut nos odio digni simus: ille mansuetudine et misericordia dignus est" (Although we merit His hatred, He is worthy of clemency and mercy); Goletti, *De otio religioso*, 76–77; Schearer, *On Religious Leisure*, 39. *Dvs.* 1.5: "Sed ita nos aspicit ut, indignos licet inveniat, misereatur tamen" (But he looks at us in such a way that, although he finds us unworthy, he nevertheless takes pity on us); Martellotti, *De vita solitaria*, 64.

76. *Secretum*: "Que [scil. vires animi], quanquam grandia et qualia tibi fingis essent, non in superbiam tamen sed in humilitatem inducere debuissent, memorantem nullis tuis meritis illa tibi singularia contigisse" (But even if these qualities were as great and as fine as you imagine, they should lead you not to pride but to humility, remembering that it is through no merit of yours that each one of them has been given to you). As it has been noted (Fenzi, *Secretum*, 319–20 n. 14), this may be a reference to Paul, 1 Cor. 4.7: "quid habes quod non accepisti? Si autem accepisti, quid gloriaris quasi non acceperis?" (What do you have that you did not receive? And if you received it, why do you boast as if you did not receive?). Fenzi, *Secretum*, 144; Mann, *My Secret Book*, 66–67. Cited also in *Dor.* (ed. Goletti, 240; ed. Schearer, 138). *Fam.* 16.4.5: "gratis me amasti, indignum melioribus pretulisti" (For no reason have you loved me, your preferred me, unworthy as I am); *Le familiari*, 3:183; *Letters on Familiar Matters*, 2:298.

77. *Secretum*: "Quid de me sperem non habeo: spes mea Deus est" (I have nothing to hope for in myself; my hope is in God); Fenzi, *Secretum*, 142; Mann, *My Secret Book*, 64–65; *Rvf.* 365.14: "tu sai ben che 'n altrui non ò speranza" (You know well that I have no hope in anyone else); Durling, *Petrarch's Lyric Poems*, 574–75. See Fenzi, *Secretum*, 318 n. 3; Rico, *Vida u obra de Petrarca*, 123; see also psalm 5.3. On the theme of *ingratitudo*, present in the Petrarchian psalms, worth noting is that God loves the ungrateful as well. See Lk. 6.35: "quia ipse benignus est super ingratos et malos" (for He himself is kind to the ungrateful and the wicked). On God's infinite mercy, see *Sen.* 10.1; and Luciani, *Les Confessions*, 230–33.

Psalm V

78. Job 4.13–14: "In horrore visionis nocturnae quando solet sopor occupare homines, pavor tenuit me et tremor et omnia ossa mea perterrita sunt" (Amid thoughts from visions of the night, when deep sleep falls on mortals, dread came upon me and trembling, which made all my bones shake); 7.14: "terrebis me per somnia et per visiones horrore concuties" (then you scare me with dreams and terrify me with visions); Ps. 90.5 (91.5): "non timebis a timore nocturno" (You will not fear the terror of the night); *De remediis*, 11.87 (Carraud, 1:916–17; Rawski, 3:203). See also the chapter of *De sompniis* in *Rerum memorandarum libri*. 4.40. On restlessness at night, see psalm 2.13–17.

79. The theme of the *amaritudo animae* is closely modeled on Job 9.18: "Non concedit requiescere spiritum meum et implet me amaritudinibus" (he will not let me get my breath but fills me with bitterness); 10.1: "Taedet animam meam vitae meae, dimittam adversum me eloquium meum, loquar in amaritudine animae meae" (I loathe my life; I will give free utterance to my complaint; I will speak in the bitterness of my soul), which in turn resonates in the "in amaritudine loquor mee menti" (I will speak in the bitterness of my mind) of the popular *Estuans intrinsecus* or the Archpoet's Confession, *Carmina Burana* 191. See David A. Traill, *Carmina Burana* (Cambridge, MA: Harvard University Press, 2018). See also Lam. 3.15: "Replevit me amaritudinibus" (He has filled me with bitterness).

80. *Rvf.* 15.2: "col corpo stancho ch' a gran pena porto" (with my weary body which with great effort I carry forward); Durling, *Petrarch's Lyric Poems*, 50–51; *Secretum*: "vetus hec curarum sarcina" (lay aside this old load of concerns); Fenzi, *Secretum*, 234; Mann, *My Secret Book*, 190–91. See also Fenzi, *Secretum*, 382 n. 186, for whom *sarcina* as "weight of the body" is typically Augustinian. *Fam.* 2.1.18: "hanc corporum sarcinam" (this burdensome body); *Le familiari*,

1:57–58; *Letters on Familiar Matters*, 1:60. *Oratio quotidiana*, in "Petrarch's Prayers" in this volume: "sarcina carnalium voluptatum exue me miserum" (strip me, miserable that I am, of the burden of the pleasures of the flesh); Ps. 37.7 (38.6): "adflictus sum et incurvatus nimis" (I am utterly bowed down and prostrate). See Giuliana Crevatin, "L'ultimo viaggio di Ariovisto: Un percorso intertestuale," in *Studi offerti a Luigi Blasucci* (Lucca: Pacini, 1996), 223–30, 229; Luciani, *Les Confessions*, 54–55, 191. In *Rvf.* 81.1 instead the burden is represented by the passions: "Io son sì stanco sotto il fascio antico de le mie colpe" (I am so weary under the ancient bundle of my sins); Durling, *Petrarch's Lyric Poems*, 185.

81. Micah 7.6: "inimici hominis domestici eius" (your enemies are members of your own household). See also Mt. 10.36.

82. Cant. 5.7: "Invenerunt me custodes qui circumeunt civitatem percusserunt me vulneraverunt me tulerunt pallium meum mihi custodes murorum" (Making their rounds in the city the sentinels found me; they beat me; they wounded me; they took away my mantle, those sentinels of the walls). See Petrarch's following psalm characterized by the theme of successful assailors. On spiritual enemies both external and internal, see *Fam.* 19.16.11: "O nascentium sors immitis, semper in prelio stare non adversus alienigenas tantum hostes sed adversus indigenas, seque ipsos et ancipiti experientia omne tempus absumere" (O cruel fate of those born to this life, to do constant battle not only against foreign enemies but internal ones and to waste their limited time on uncertain self-trials); *Le familiari*, 3:343; *Letters on Familiar Matters*, 3:108. On the militaristic metaphor, see, e.g., *Dor.*: "Tunc enim plena securitas certaque demum pax speranda vobis est, quando fortiter atque feliciter exacta militia vite huius ab exilio in patriam, e castris in regnum atque in regiam veri regis eritis translati et facti de laboriosis militibus veterani emeriti, succedente premio labori" (You may hope to have complete security and guaranteed peace when, having courageously and successfully completed your military life, you will be taken from this exile into your homeland, from military camps into the kingdom and into the palace of the true king. At that time you will be transformed from soldiers *in service* into veterans who have served with distinction); Goletti, *De otio religioso*, 49; Schearer, *On Religious Leisure*, 23 (translation in italics mine, which replaces Schearer "diligent," in light of the connotations that *labor* takes in the psalms). See also Goletti, *De otio religioso*, 188; and Schearer, *On Religious Leisure*, 106, where our flesh is considered the "domestic enemy" against which we should do battle. *Dvs.* 1.9: "Alii regant urbem populi, alii militum exercitum, et nobis urbs animi nostri est, nostrarum exercitus curarum: bellis civilibus et externis quatimur" (May other cities of the people, other armies of soldiers rule: we have the city of our soul, the army of our troubles: internal and external wars disturb us); Martellotti, *De vita solitaria*,

118–19. See also *Fam.* 20.1.15, which elaborates on the metaphor of the assault on the walls: "scale criminum parietibus animarum" (the ladder of crime against the walls of the soul); *Le familiari*, 4:6; *Letters on Familiar Matters*, 3:124–25.

83. *Ep. metr.* 1.14.6: "optate non spes patet ulla salutis" (nowhere is the prospect of the longed-for salvation); *Eclogue* 9.27–28; Pierre De Nolhac mentions *De remediis*, 1.33, and sees Catullus (64.186) as possible source: "nulla fugae ratio, nulla spes" (no means of flight, no hope). *Pétrarque et l'humanisme*, 2 vols. (Paris: Champion, 1907), 1:169. However, on Catullus as possible source, see Duane Reed Stuart's "Petrarch's Indebtedness to the *Libellus* of Catullus," *TAPA* 48 (1917): 3–26. At any rate, Catullus has the "quid faciam" topos to recommend itself as direct target of allusion in this context (pace Duane Reed Stuart). In Matthieu de Vendome's *Tobias*, "fuga nulla patet." See Giuseppe Velli, "Petrarca e la grande poesia latina del XII secolo," *Italia medievale e umanistica* 28 (1985): 295–310, at 309.

84. Ps. 12.6 (13.5): "Ego autem in misericordia tua confido" (But I trusted in your steadfast love).

85. *Oratio quotidiana*, in "Petrarch's Prayers" in this volume: "Age iam, propera, festina, accelera, eripe me, predulcis Ihesu, de laqueo hostis mei et de faucibus hostis huius" (So do not delay, make haste, hurry and deliver me, quickly, sweet Jesus, from the snare of my enemy and from the jaws of this death); Ps. 30.3 (31.2): "Inclina ad me aurem tuam velociter libera me" (Incline your ear to me; rescue me speedily).

Psalm VI

86. Ps. 16.9–11 (17.9): "Inimici mei animam meam circumdederunt" (my deadly enemies who surround me); Ps. 55.3 (56.2): "Conculcaverunt me insidiatores mei tota die" (my enemies trample on me all day long); Ps. 142.3 (143.3): "persecutus est enim inimicus animam meam confregit in terra vitam meam posuit me in tenebris quasi mortuos antiquos" (For the enemy has pursued me, crushing my life to the ground, making me sit in darkness like those long dead). See the allegorization in the *Africa* 5.402–4: "turba voluptatum que circumfusa tenet nos" (the multitude of pleasures that surrounds us). In *L'Africa: Edizione critica*, 117. The same recourse to images of assault and combat recalls the *Secretum*. See Casali, "Petrarca 'penitenziale,'" 377; and Rico, *Vida u obra de Petrarca*, 124. See also the beginning of *Fam.* 7.12.1: "Heu, quid hoc est? quid audio; O spes mortalium fallax, o cure supervacue, o labilis status! nichil homini tranquillum,

nichil stabile, nichil tutum; hinc fortune vis, hinc mortis insidie, hinc fugacis mundi blanditie: undique circonvallamur miseri" (Alas, what has happened? What do I hear? Oh deceitful hope of mortals, oh useless cares, oh precarious human condition! There is nothing peaceful for humankind, nothing stable, nothing safe: here we see the power of fortune, there the traps of death, and there the flattery of the fleeing world: on every side we are surrounded by wretchedness); *Le familiari*, 2:117; *Letters on Familiar Matters*, 1:361.

87. Ps. 54.5–6 (55.4–5): "Cor meum doluit in vitalibus meis et terrores mortis ceciderunt super me. Timor et tremor venit super me, et operuit me caligo" (My heart is in anguish within me; the terrors of death have fallen upon me. Fear and trembling come upon me, and horror overwhelms me); and Ps. 43.20 (44.19): "et operuisti nos umbra mortis" (and covered us with deep darkness).

88. *Rvf.* 81.3: "ch'i' temo forte di mancar tra via" (that I am much afraid I shall to fail on the way); 264.12–13: "ché chi, possendo star, cadde tra via / degno è che mal suo grado a terra giaccia" (for he who, able to stand, has fallen along the way deserves to lie on the ground against his will); Durling, *Petrarch's Lyric Poems*, 184–85 and 426–27, respectively. 1 Cor. 10.12: "Itaque qui se existimat stare videat ne cadat" (So if you think you are standing, watch out that you do not fall). The expression *pronus in terram* in the Old Testament is used to express the deepest and humblest adoration toward God. See Gn. 17.3; Ex. 34.8; Nm. 16.4; Joshua 5.15: "Cecidit Iosue pronus in terram" (And Joshua fell on his face to the earth). In Ps. 70.3 (71.3), God is "petra mea et fortitudo mea es tu" (be to me a rock of refuge). The theme of a spiritual fall (see in particular the following psalm) as separation from God is well established since Augustine's *Soliloquia* 1.3: "Deus, a quo averti cadere, in quem converti resurgere, in quo manere consistere est" (God, from whom to turn away is to fall, to whom to turn toward is to rise again, in whom to remain is to stand firm). The introductory prayer of the *Soliloquia*, i.e., 1.2–6, is clearly a source for Petrarch. The English translation is from *Soliloquies: Augustine's Inner Dialogue*, ed. John E. Rotelle, trans. Kim Paffenroth, and introd. Boniface Ramsey (Hyde Park, NY: New City Press, 2000), 21. It is of course a very widespread spiritual topos. *Carmina Burana* 29.3: "Ut stes pede stabili / sine casu facili, / cave precipitium, / devitando vitium" (So that you stand on a firm foot / without an easy fall, / beware of the precipice, / avoiding injury).

89. Ps. 55.3 (56.1): "Conculcaverunt me insidiatores mei tota die" (my enemies trample on me all day long).

90. Lk. 10.30: "Homo quidam . . . incidit in latrones qui etiam despoliaverunt eum et plagis impositis abierunt semivivo relicto" (A man . . . fell into the hands of robbers, who stripped him, beat him, and took off, leaving him half dead).

91. Cicero, *Tusc.* 1.10.20: "Plato . . . cupiditatem supter praecordia locavit" (Plato . . . placed desire under the chest), recalled in *Fam.* 12.14.2. The verb *debacchari* appears in accounts of martyrs in relation to the furious rage of executioners (as seen later in this psalm). See also Pier Damiani, *Sermo* 22.4: "brachia [scil. carnificum] quae in ictus debacchantur" (whose arms [of the executionary] go wild in blows). The Latin text is available at CC, https://mlat.uzh.ch/browser?path=/38&text=10048.

92. Ps. 37.6 (38.5): "Conputruerunt et tabuerunt cicatrices meae a facie insipientiae meae" (My wounds grow foul and fester because of my foolishness); *Fam.* 10.5.27: "abditas scelerum meorum sordes, que funesta segnitie longoque silentio putruerant . . . ; omnipotenti medico cecum animi mei vulnus ostendere" (the base ugliness of my sins, which had rotted in fatal sluggishness and long silence . . . revealing the blind wounds of my soul to the almighty Healer); *Le familiari*, 2:317; *Letters on Familiar Matters*, 1:81. See also *Secretum*: "Heu mi misero! Nunc profunde manum in vulnus adegisti. Istic dolor meus inhabitat, istinc mortem metuo." (What a wretched state I'm in! Now you have plunged your hand deep into the wound. Here is the seat of my suffering, this is why I fear death); Fenzi, *Secretum*, 140; Mann, *My Secret Book*, 62–63. The image of *putredo* is emblematic of Job's affliction. Job 7.5: "Induta est caro mea putredine" (My flesh is clothed with worms and dirt); 13.28: "Qui quasi putredo consumendus sum" (One wastes away like a rotten thing); 25.6: "quanto magis homo putredo et filius hominis vermis" (how much less a mortal, who is a maggot, and a human being, who is a worm!). However, the same macabre language is present in classical authors like Statius. See *Theb.* 3.582–84: "tunc fessa putri robigine pila / haerentesque situ gladios in saeua recurant / uulnera et attrito cogunt iuuenescere saxo" (refurbishing the pikes tarnished with rust, / swords sheathed in their neglected scabbards, grinding them / to render them new again, ready to deal out cruel wounds). The Latin text is available at CC, https://mlat.uzh.ch/browser?path=12770&text=12770:3.

93. Ps. 13.2 (14.2): "Dominus de caelo prospexit super filios hominum" (The Lord looks down from heaven on humankind).

94. Is. 42.14: "Tacui semper silui patiens fui" (For a long time I have held my peace; I have kept still and restrained myself).

95. Ps. 73.19 (74.19): "vitae pauperum tuorum ne obliviscaris in perpetuum" (do not forget the life of your poor forever), also cited in Petrarch's *Liber sine nomine* 12.19. See *Liber sine nomine*, trans. Laura Casarsa (Turin: Aragno, 2010), 112–13. Ps. 9.19 (9.18): "Quoniam non in aeternum oblivioni erit pauper" (But God will never forget the needy).

96. Ps. 7.2 (7.1): "Domine Deus meus in te speravi salva me ab omnibus persequentibus me et libera me" (O Lord my God, in you I take refuge; save me from all my pursuers and deliver me).

Psalm VII

97. Prv. 4.19: "Via impiorum tenebrosa nesciunt ubi corruant" (The way of the wicked is like deep darkness; they do not know what they stumble over), also cited in *Fam.* 7.17.2.

98. "Allisus sum" from *allido*, means "to have been injured, damaged." However, considering the port and storm imagery following in v. 5, "shipwrecked" is consistent with the Petrarchan *navigatio* metaphor present here and elsewhere. On this topic, see psalm 1.8 and 9. See also *Dvs.* 2.14: "fugiamus, oro, iantandem et id quantulumcunque quod superest in solitudine transigamus, omni studio caventes, ne, dum opem ferre naufragiis videmur, ipsi rerum humanarum fluctibus obruamur, scopulis allidamur (let us flee, I pray you, and let us spend in solitude whatever little time remains, taking care with all diligence lest, while we are seen to bring aid to the shipwrecked, we ourselves be not overwhelmed by the waves of human affairs, and be dashed against the rocks). Martellotti, *De vita solitaria*, 284–85.

99. See also *Dvs.* 1.4: "in medio tempestatis portum michi conflare didicerim" (a port in the midst of solitude I know how to create for myself) even though the circumstances are quite different. Martellotti, *De vita solitaria*, 52–53.

100. Augustine, *Sermo* 225.3: "adhuc cogitatio humana erret per nebulas suas" (Let human thought still go on wandering through its cloudy spheres). The English translation is from Augustine, *Sermons 184–229Z*, in *The Works of Saint Augustine: A Translation for the 21st Century*, III/6:248.

101. *Fam.* 7.17.12: "quamque error ambiguus per inextricabiles vite brevis anfractus" (how uncertain is the wandering through the tortuous windings of this brief life); *Le familiari*, 2:135; *Letters on Familiar Matters*, 1:382. See again *Dvs.* 1.4: "per devia raptamur . . . , sepe periculosas et inexplicabiles ingredimur vias" (we let ourselves be dragged along treacherous roads . . . , we set out along winding and intricate paths); Martellotti, *De vita solitaria*, 48–49.

102. In *Fam.* 24.1.25 on the *de inextimabili fuga temporis*, Petrarch writes: "Ego ipse michi placui, me dilexi; nunc, quid dicam? odi. Sed mentiar: nemo unquam carnem suam odio habuit. Dicam: 'non me diligo'; id quoque quam vere sim dicturus, nescio. Illud intrepide dixerim: 'non diligo peccatum meum neque

mores meos diligo, nisi quia mutati in melius correctique sunt.' Imo, quid hesitem? et peccatum et mores malos et me ipsum talem odi; ab Augustino enim didici neminem fieri posse qualis cupit, nisi se oderit qualis est" (I used to take pleasure in myself, I loved myself. What shall I say about now? I hate myself. But I am lying; no one ever felt hatred for his own flesh. Shall I say, 'I do not love myself?' I do not know how true that may be either. This much I can say with assurance, 'I do not love my sins, nor do I love my ways except insofar as they have changed for the better and improved.' But why hesitate? I hate my sinfulness, my evil habits, and myself as I am, for I learned from Augustine that no one can become what he wishes unless he hates himself as he is); *Le familiari*, 4:219–20; *Letters on Familiar Matters*, 3:312. Petrarch may well refer here to Augustine's *De vera religione* 88 where the painful hatred of oneself is only beneficial if it is symptomatic of a change for the better: the *novus homo* hates *the vetus homo*.

103. *Africa* 7.673–74: "Multa quoniam pietate coactus / vim patior" (I suffer many things because I am compelled by pity); see also Marco Baglio, "Presenze dantesche nel Petrarca latino," *Studi petrarcheschi* 9 (1992): 77–136, 108 n. 44.

104. *Rvf.* 264.136: "et veggio 'l meglio, et al peggior m'appiglio" (and I see the better but I lay hold of the worse); Durling, *Petrarch's Lyric Poems*, 432–33; see also 236.1–4; Rom. 7.15, 20: "non enim quod volo hoc ago sed quod odi illud facio. . . . Non enim quod volo bonum hoc facio sed quod nolo malum hoc ago" (For I do not do what I want, but I do the very thing I hate. . . . For I do not do the good I want, but I do the evil I do not want), cited in *Fam.* 17.10.10–11; Ovid, *Metamorphoses*, 7.20–21: "video meliora proboque, / deteriora sequor" (I see a better way and approve it, but I follow the worst way). The Latin text is available at CC, https://www.mlat.uzh.ch/browser?path=12563&text=12724:7. See Goletti, "Volentes unum aliud agimus," 79; and Martinelli, *Il "Secretum" conteso*, 189, 269.

105. Prv. 26.11: "Sicut canis qui revertitur ad vomitum suum" (Like a dog that returns to its vomit); and 2 Pet. 2.22. The same expression recurs in *De sui ipsius*; see Marsh, *Invectives*, 288–89.

106. Gal. 6.3: "Nam si quis existimat se aliquid esse cum sit nihil ipse se seducit" (For if those who are nothing think they are something, they deceive themselves). See also Pliny the Elder, who in *Naturalis Historiae* 11.138 writes, "Haec maxime indicant fastum, Superbia aliubi conceptaculum, sed hic sedem habet" (Arrogance is conceived elsewhere, but has its home here: it is born in the heart, but comes to the brow and lingers there). The Latin text is available at CC, https://www.mlat.uzh.ch/browser?path=12344.

107. 2 Pet. 1.19: "Et habemus firmiorem propheticum sermonem cui bene facitis adtendentes quasi lucernae lucenti in caliginoso loco donec dies inlucescat et lucifer oriatur in cordibus vestris" (So we have the prophetic message more fully confirmed. You will do well to be attentive to this as to a lamp shining in a dark place, until the day dawns and the morning star rises in your hearts), cited also in Augustine's *Enarrationes in psalmos*, 142.14.

108. "Praesumptio spiritus" (presumption of spirit) in Ecclesiastes 6.9; "praesumptionem cordis" (presumption of the heart) in Ecclesiasticus 18.10 and 37.3: "O praesumptio nequissima" (O inclination to evil).

109. *Secretum*: "Signum tamen aliquod memorie mee, si videtur, imprime, quo admonitus post hac de me ipse michi non mentiar, nec erroribus meis interblandiar" (Please impress upon my memory some sign that will remind me from now onward not to deceive myself about myself, and not to indulge my errors); Fenzi, *Secretum*, 124; Mann, *My Secret Book*, 46–47. See Petrarch's psalm 1: "in peccatis michi blanditus sum" (and in my sins I flattered myself).

110. Ps. 2.11: "Servite Domino in timore et exultate ei in tremore" (Serve the Lord with fear; with trembling), recalled also in *Fam.* 10.3.58 and in *Dor.* 2. 4–5. The expression "Fear and trembling" appears frequently in the Bible. See 1 Cor. 2.3, Eph. 6.5, Phil. 2.12, and Ps. 54.6 (55.6): "Timor et tremor venit super me et operuit me caligo" (Fear and trembling come upon me, and horror overwhelms me).

111. *Rvf.* 294.12: "Veramente siam noi polvere et ombra" (Truly, we are dust and shadow); 133.2–3: "come al sol neve, come cera al foco / et come nebbia al vento" (like snow in the sun, like wax in the fire, like a cloud in the wind); 319.1–2: "I dí miei più leggier' che nesun cervo / fuggir come ombra" (My days, swifter than any deer, have fled like a shadow) (see Baglio, "Presenze dantesche nel Petrarca latino," 78; see also *Triumphus Aeternitatis*, 66); 331.22: "Nebbia o polvere al vento" (A cloud or dust in the wind); Durling, *Petrarch's Lyric Poems*, 472–73, 270–71, 498–99, 520–21. *Africa* 2.348–50: "umbra / umbra estis pulvisque levis vel in ethere fumus / exiguus, quem ventus agat" (a shadow, you are a shadow and light dust, or a little smoke in the air, which the wind blows). *L'Africa: Edizione critica*, 43. *Rerum Memorandarum* 3.80.12–13: "limus et umbra tenuis sumus et fumus euro volvente rarissimus" (We are mud and fading shadow, rarefied smoke as the Eurus blows); the Latin citation is from *Rerum Memorandarum Libri*, ed. Marco Petoletti (Florence: Le Lettere, 2014), 326–27. *Fam.* 1.2.29: "ventus est fama quam sequimur, fumus est umbra est, nichil est" (The fame we seek is but a breeze, smoke a shadow: it is nothing); *Fam.* 11.3.10: "video eam ipsam que vita dicitur, fugacis umbram nebule vel fumum ventis impulsum

denique vel confusum somnium esse vel fabulam inexpletam vel siquid inanius dici potest" (I see that even what is called life is but a shadow of a fleeting cloud, or smoke wafted by the winds, or finally troubled sleep or an unfinished tale or anything else conceivably more empty); *Le familiari*, 1:21, 2:328; *Letters on Familiar Matters*, 1:21; 2:90. *Sen.* 1.5.16: "fumus umbra, somnium . . . vita est" (Indeed the life we live here is only smoke, a shadow, a dream, an illusion); *Ep. metr.* 1.14.83: "cum pulvis ero" (when dust I will be); Horace, *Ode* 4.7.16: "pulvis et umbra sumus" (dust and shadow we are); Ps. 101.4 (102.3): "Quia defecerunt sicut fumus dies mei" (For my days pass away like smoke), and v. 11: "Dies mei sicut umbra declinaverunt" (My days are like a lengthening shadow); Ps. 143.4 (144.4): "dies eius sicut umbra praetereunt" (their days are like a passing shadow); Ps. 17.43 (18.42): "Et comminuam illos ut pulverem ante faciem venti" (I beat them fine, like dust before the wind); Ps. 34.5 (35.5): "tamquam pulvis ante faciem venti" (like chaff before the wind); Wisdom 2.5: "Umbrae enim transitus est tempus nostrum" (For our allotted time is the passing of a shadow), 5.9: "tamquam umbra" (like a shadow), and 15: "tamquam fumus qui a vento diffusus est" (it is dispersed like smoke before the wind); Job 8.9: "sicut umbra dies nostri sunt super terram" (for our days on earth are but a shadow), 14.2: "fugit velut umbra" (flees like a shadow), from which "fugit, transit velut umbra" (flees like a shadow passes), *Carmina Burana*, 24.6; Augustine, *Confessions* 1.17: "Non ecce illa omnia fumus et ventus?" (Actually, was not all that smoke and wind?); In Johann. evang. tract., 10.6: "Nonne omnia fumus et ventus?" (Isn't everything smoke and wind?). Moreover, man "pulvis est" (is dust), as in Gn. 2.7: "formavit igitur Dominus Deus hominem de limo terrae" (the Lord God formed man from the dust of the ground); see also Gn. 3.19 (repeated in Ps. 102.14 and, along with Job 14.2, cited in *Dvs.* 1.4). As a symbolic image of decay, smoke, wind, and shadow recur regularly in many passages of patristic literature. See Gauthier De Saint-Victor, *Sermo* 13.4: "mundi gaudium . . . mox desinit et evanescit tanquam fumus, tanquam ventus et sicut umbra" (the joy of the world . . . soon ends and vanishes like smoke, like wind and like a shadow). As Gigliucci aptly observes, Petrarch here hybridizes the Horatian couplet *pulvis-umbra* (from *Ode* 4.7) with *limus-pulvis* from Genesis, thus opting for "limus et umbra," which perfectly exemplifies Petrarch's classical-Christian cultural blending.

    112. For the polyptoton (reinforced by "videar" in the following line), see, e.g., *Fam.* 20.2.5: "videor videre" (I seem to see). Similar rhetorical expressions appear often in the Bible and Latin Christian poetry (e.g., "sanctum sanctorum"), but occurrences of "videor videre," "video videri," are also frequent in Cicero and other classical authors; see Terence, *Adelphoe*, 384; Seneca, *De Beneficiis*, 7.27; Plautus, *Epidicus*, 1.62.

113. Ps. 16.8 (17.8): "in umbra alarum tuarum" (in the shadow of your wings); Ps. 62.8 (63.7): "in umbra alarum tuarum laudabo" (in the shadow of your wings I sing for joy) recalled by Petrarch in an autographed marginal note in Vat. Lat. 458, containing the works of Augustine. See Giuseppe Billanovich, "Dalle prime alle ultime letture del Petrarca," in *Il Petrarca ad Arquà* (Padua: Antenore, 1975), 13–50, at 46. Worth noting is the stark contrast between the steady and secure *umbra* found under the divine wings and the very fragile *umbra* of which man is made.

114. The theme of mockery, persecution, and derision is typically biblical, and in the Old Testament it figuratively foreshadows Christ's passion. See in particular the prophetic books: Lam. 3.14: "factus sum in derisu omni populo meo canticum eorum tota die" (I have become the laughingstock of all my people, the object of their taunt songs all day long); Jer. 20.7: "factus sum in derisum tota die omnes subsannant me" (I have become a laughingstock all day long; everyone mocks me); and especially Isaiah (The Suffering Servant: 52.13–53.12). For the Psalms, see 21.8 (22.7): "omnes videntes me subsannant me" (All who see me mock me; they sneer at me; they shake their heads), 68.12 (69.11): "et factus sum eis in parabulam" (I became a byword to them). But exquisitely Petrarchan is precisely the theme of being *vulgi fabula* (see *Rvf.* 1.10, *Secretum* 3.182 in Fenzi's edition, p. 250); see also 392 n. 268 for other references), frequent throughout Petrarch's work and already present in classical *auctores* (see Horace, *Epodon* 11.7–8; and Ovid, *Amores*, 3.1.19–21). See also Marco Santagata's commentary on *Rvf.* 1.10, in the *Canzoniere* (Milan: Mondadori, 1996), 10–12.

115. *Dor.*: "Nichil impossibile Deo est; in me est omnis impossibilitas assurgendi tanta peccatorum mole obruto" (Nothing is impossible for God; all the impossibility of rising up from so great a burden of sins is on me); Goletti, *De otio religioso*, 72; Schearer, *On Religious Leisure*, 37.

116. Ps. 5.7 (5.6): "virum sanguinum et dolosum abominabitur Dominus" (the Lord abhors the bloodthirsty and deceitful); Ps. 50.16 (51.14): "libera me de sanguinibus" (deliver me from bloodshed); Ps. 54.24 (55.23): "viri sanguinum et dolosi" (the bloodthirsty and treacherous); Ps. 58.3 (59.2): "de viris sanguinum salva me" (from the bloodthirsty, save me); Jn. 1.13: "qui non ex sanguinibus neque ex voluntate carnis neque ex voluntate viri sed ex Deo nati sunt" (who were born, not of blood or of the will of the flesh or of the will of man, but of God). Flesh and blood are of course symbols of corruptibility and transience in Ecclesiasticus 14.18–19. For the expression *versari in sanguinibus*, see Augustine, *De civitate dei* 4.3: "cum hominum felicitatem non possis ostendere, semper in bellicis cladibus et in sanguine civili vel hostili, tamen humano cum tenebroso timore et cruenta cupiditate versantium" (you cannot show that its [Rome's] people are

happy . . . [who] always dwell in the midst of the disasters of war and the spilling of blood—the blood of fellow citizens or the blood of foreign enemies, but in either case human blood—and always live under the dark shadow of fear and the lust for blood). The English translation is from *The City of God*, in *The Works of Saint Augustine: A Translation for the Twenty-First Century*, introd. and trans. William Babcock (Hyde Park, NY: New City Press, 1990), I/6:111. The syntagm is however already classical; see Sallust, *The Jugurthine War*, 14; and Cicero, *Pro Roscio Amerino*, 29. According to Cochin, "versor in sanguinibus" alludes to sensuality and the flesh; see Cochin, *Les Psaumes Pénitentiaux*, 115. Of the same opinion is Casali; see "Petrarca 'penitenziale,'" 368.

117. Ps. 39.3 (40.2): "eduxit me de lacu famoso et de luto caeni" (he drew me up from the desolate pit, out of the miry bog); Ps. 68.15 (69.14): "erue me de luto ut non infingar" (rescue me from sinking in the mire); Augustine, *Enarrationes* 39.3: "Quis est lacus miseriae? Profunditas iniquitatis, ex carnalibus concupiscentiis. Hoc est enim 'et de luto limi'" (What is this pit of misery? The murky depth of iniquity to which carnal lusts consign us). The English translation is from *Expositions of the Psalms 33–50*, in *The Works of Saint Augustine: A Translation for the 21st Century*, III/16:197. Petrarch knew Augustine's *Enarrationes* (the ones before Ps. 101) perhaps not before 1355; see Giuseppe Billanovich, "Nella biblioteca del Petrarca: Il Petrarca, il Boccaccio e le 'Enarrationes in Psalmos' di S. Agostino," *Italia medioevale e umanistica* 3 (1960): 3–27. In the *Moralia in Iob*, 34.15, Gregory the Great elucidates the symbolic meanings, "in sacro eloquio" (in sacred speech), of the term *lutum*: "Per lutum quoque desiderium sordidae voluptatis exprimitur, sicut psalmista deprecans ait: 'Eripe me de luto, ut non inhaeream.' Luto quippe inhaerere est sordidis desideriis concupiscentiae carnalis inquinari" (The desire for filthy pleasure is also expressed through mud, as the psalmist says in supplication: 'Deliver me from the mud, that I may not stick to it.' For to cling to mud is to be defiled by the sordid desires of carnal concupiscence). Hence, see *Fam*. 4.12.29: "carnis nostrae tenacissimo limo ac sordibus hereamus" (to cling to the thick filth and to the dregs of our flesh); and 5.18.2: "undique me habent angustie in luto carnis et in vinculis mortalitatis mee adhuc aut sedentem aut iacentem" (human distress hold me thus far either sitting or lying in the mire of the flesh and in the chains of my mortality); *Le familiari* 1:184, 2:42; *Letters on Familiar Matters*, 1:207, 276.

118. Virgil uses the neuter plural *extrema* in the sense of "death, end of life"; see *Aeneid* 6.457.

PETRARCH'S PRAYERS

ORATIONES
(Par. Lat. 2201)

I.
1335, die 1 iunii.
1. Tibi, Domine Ihesu Christe, creator mirifice et amator munifice humani generis, tibi, unica salus et vita mea, per quem sum, in quo sum et sine quo nichil sum, a quo presente longe absum, tibi, inquam, soli, Salvator optime, anime mee ac corporis, munerum tuorum, committo custodiam, ut eorum societatem illibatam et tibi placidam efficias, ne corrumpantur ex alterutro, neve ex concretione mortali aut illud tyrannidem solitam exerceat, aut illa servitutis ultime iugum perferat, sed secundum placitum tuum illud serviat, illa dominetur, tibi tamen pariter militent et, abiecta contumaci superbia, obediant usque in finem. 2. Divitias aut paupertatem in hac vita ac ceterarum rerum temporalium affluentiam vel defectum non postulo: quod enim saluti mee convenientius sit nemo novit preter te; in secundis sane modestiam, in adversis rebus fortem animum et patientiam presta. 3. Tibi, Deus meus, commendo cogitationes et actus meos, tibi silentium et sermones, tibi motus et quietem, tibi dies et noctes, tibi sompnum et vigilias, tibi risum et lacrimas, tibi spes et desideria, tibi vite mee tempus et mortis horam, ad quam te flebilius invoco et humilius deprecor ut michi adesse digneris in tempore opportuno, oblitus iniquitatum mearum, quarum tamen immemorem nulla me faciat dies. 4. Pudorem ac dolorem tantis condignum erroribus infunde celitus, rex celorum; tange lapidem cordis mei, unde exeant fontes lacrimarum quibus abluantur peccatorum meorum vulnera que te spectante michi ipse intuli, miserrimus et proprie salutis inimicus; sana me, qui solus potes. 5. Quid enim ego sine te? Scis tu, Domine, qui omnia respicis, et ego, infelix homo, testis factus imbecillitatis mee, in me ipso aliqua iam ex parte recognosco: hoc quoque tu facis, hoc ut uberius efficias queso, ne quid de me ipso confisus, spem totam iaciam in te, ut orare sciam et exorare te merear. 6. Audi vocem meam indignam ad aures tuas pervenire; vide, Ihesu, infirmitatem meam et langorem animi ulcerosi et miserere; concupiscentias obliquas aufer a me, et sarcina carnalium voluptatum exue me miserum antequam moriar et cum omnibus malis meis descendam ad inferos, heu,

Petrarch's Autograph Prayers
(in *Par. Lat. 2201*)

I.
June 1, 1335

1. To you, Lord Jesus Christ, wonderful creator and munificent lover of mankind, to you, only salvation and my life, for whom I am, in whom I am and without whom I am nothing, from whom, though present, I am long absent, to you alone, I say, my Savior, I entrust the safe-keeping of my soul and body, your gifts, so that you may make their union intact and pleasing to you, so they may not corrupt each other, out of their mortiferous conjunction, and so that neither the body may exercise its customary tyranny, nor the soul may bear the yoke of the worst kind of slavery, but, as pleases you, let the body serve and the soul rule, and also let both equally fight for you, and, rejecting the arrogance of pride, obey you always until the end.[1] 2. I do not ask for wealth or poverty in this life nor for abundance or shortage of other temporal goods: no one knows but you what in fact is most appropriate for my salvation; grant me, therefore, moderation in prosperity and fortitude and patience in adversity. 3. To you, my God, I entrust my thoughts and my actions, my silence and words, my actions and rest, my days and nights, my sleep and wakefulness, my laughter and tears, my hopes and desires, the time of my life and the hour of my death, at which I tearfully invoke and humbly beg that you deign to be present for me, when the time comes, forgetting my iniquities, of which, however, I am mindful every single day. 4. King of Heaven, instill in me from above a shame and pain commensurate with such great errors; touch the stone of my heart, from which founts of tears may emerge to cleanse the wounds of my sins, which I inflicted on myself as you watched.[2] As I am most wretched and the enemy of my own health, heal me; for only you can.[3] 5. For what am I without you? You know it, Lord, as you see everything. I, too, understand it in some part of myself, as I am a wretched man, made a witness of my weakness. This too is your work, and I ask you to make this awareness ever deeper, so that, without trusting in myself, all my hope will be in you, and that I may know how to pray, so that my prayers may be answered. 6. Listen to my unworthy voice that reaches your

nunquam reversurus! 7. Libera me de manibus inimicorum meorum qui me trahunt precipitem; erue animam meam ex hoc tartaro, ubi eam vivendo sponte demersi; aspice vulnera que pro salute mea pertulisti, tantoque redemptum pretio ludibrium Sathane ne linquas; manus et latus et pedes tuos consule, et dicent tibi ne sacrum tui corporis sanguinem frustra michi fluxisse patiaris. 8. Aperi oculos meos, sompno mortis oppressos et terrenarum sordium nube caligantes, ac lucem tuam iam tandem illis ostende; dirige gressus meos in viam pacis et per semitas mandatorum tuorum a quibus tam longe aberravi, et ne avertas faciem tuam a me. 9. De nichilo me creasti; ecce, ad nichilum relapsus sum: suscipe me, Domine Ihesu Christe, et de nichilo recrea; rem magnam, sed tibi facilem et aliis sepe concessam, efflagito: cor mundum ut crees in me, Deus, et spiritum rectum innoves in visceribus meis, recreatumque ac renovatum custodias, ne iterum revertar in nichilum. 10. Infinite bonus, infinite misericors diceris; ego autem in infinitum peccasse me fateor et infinitam venie materiam contraxisse adversus misericordiam tuam; delicta mea contendunt: raro unquam copia dabitur tam nobilis triumphi. 11. Ostende michi quam invictissimus sis, qui mortem vincentem omnia superasti; in me experire quam sis magnus, quem innumerabilia peccata mea adequare non possunt; quam fortis, a quo mens mea ferrea frangatur; quam victoriosus, cui succumbant omnes iniquitates mee; quam clarus, qui tenebras illumines cecitatis mee. 12. Incute nunc vim Spiritus Sancti et dirumpantur vincula mea; obrue acies fantasmatum quibus obsideor et illusiones demonum averte; fac me amare te ex toto corde meo et ex tota anima mea; fac me delectari in his tantum que tibi sunt accepta et odisse omnia que gravaris. 13. Passionis tue memoriam et meditationem exitus mei precordiis meis immitte, et salvum me fac, per illam ineffabilem humilitatem que te ex eterna tue maiestatis gloria traxit in terras, per illam mansuetudinem que te inclinavit ut verbum caro fieres et habitares in nobis, perque illam clementiam que te coegit ut temporaliter mori velles ne nos eterna morte moreremur. 14. Ac per omnia tui erga nos amoris insignia parce peccatori, miserere languentis, succurre obsesso, cadentem substenta, iacentem erige; ne me proculcet adversarius, solivagum Spiritus Sancti gratia circumsta, opem fer victo, deviantem revoca, fugientem retrahe, duricordem contere, cecum illustra, egrotum sana, mortuum denique suscita, qui Lazarum suscitasti. 15. Ecce, enim pereo si paululum adesse distuleris. Non tu ad quem venias, sed quis venias attende, pater et fons omnis misericordie.

ears; look, Jesus, at my infirmity and the weakness of my wounded soul, and have pity; take away the sinister lust from me, and strip me, miserable that I am, of the burden of the pleasures of the flesh, before I die and descend to the world below with all my iniquities, alas, without return![4] 7. Deliver me from the hands of my enemies, who draw me into the abyss; pluck my soul out of this Hell, where I deliberately buried it alive; look at the wounds you endured for my salvation, and do not abandon me to the mockery of Satan after having redeemed me at such a high price; ask your hands and your side and your feet, and they will tell you not to allow the sacred blood of your body to be shed in vain for me. 8. Open my eyes, oppressed by the sleep of death and blinded by the haze of earthly filth, and at last show them your light; guide my steps on the way to peace and on the paths of your commandments, from which I have strayed so far away, and do not turn your face away from me.[5] 9. You created me from nothing; see, I have returned to nothing: lift me up, Lord Jesus Christ, and re-create me from nothing; I request a great thing, but it is easy for you and often granted to others: that you create in me a pure heart,[6] my God, and renew a righteous spirit deep within me, and preserve me, re-created and renewed, so that I do not turn my path back toward nothingness. 10. You will be proclaimed infinitely good, endlessly merciful; but I confess I have sinned endlessly and have accumulated before your mercy an infinite number of causes for forgiveness; my faults resist you, but hardly ever will be offered an opportunity for such a noble triumph. 11. Show me how invincible you are, you who have overcome death that conquers all; test in me how great you are, you whose greatness far outweighs my innumerable sins; show me how strong you are, you by whom my unyielding mind can be shattered; show me how victorious you are, to whom all my iniquities succumb; show me how radiant you are, you who can bring light to the darkness of my blindness. 12. Bring down on me the power of the Holy Spirit, and let my chains be broken; crush the legion of spirits by which I am besieged and turn away the false illusions of the demons; make me love you with all my heart and with all my soul; let me delight only in what pleases you,[7] and hate everything that grieves you. 13. Put in my heart the memory of your passion and the meditation on my death. Save me,[8] in the name of that ineffable humility that brought you on earth from the eternal glory of your majesty; in the name of that kindness that led you, Word of God, to become flesh and to live among us; and in the name of that mercy that compelled you to want to

Age iam, propera, festina, accelera, eripe me, predulcis Ihesu, de laqueo hostis mei et de faucibus mortis huius. Amen.

II.
Brevior
1338, die 10 iulii.
1. Salus mea, Christe Ihesu, si te ad misericordiam inclinare potest humana miseria, adesto michi misero et preces meas benignus exaudi: fac peregrinationem meam tibi placitam et gressus meos dirige in viam salutis eterne; 2. dignare michi in die exitus mei et in illa suprema hora mortis assistere, neque reminiscaris iniquitatum mearum, sed egredientem ex hoc corpusculo spiritum placatus excipias; ne intres in iudicium cum servo tuo, Domine; 3. misericordiarum fons, misericorditer mecum age, cause mee faveas et deformitates meas contege in die novissimo, nec patiaris hanc animam, opus manuum tuarum, ad superbum tui et mei hostis imperium pervenire, aut predam fieri spiritibus immundis et famelicis canibus esse ludibrio, Deus meus, misericordia mea.

III.
Omnipotens, sempiterne Deus, ignosce metuentibus et parce supplicantibus, ut intereant noxii calores imbrium spiritusque procellarum; cedat ad honorem tue laudis comminatio tue maiestatis. Per Christum Dominum nostrum. Amen.

die temporarily, so that we might not die the eternal death. 14. And for all the signs of your love towards us, forgive me, as I am a sinner;[9] have mercy on me, for I languish; rescue me, for I am besieged; support me, for I fall; lift me up, for I am prostrate; lest the enemy trample over me, when I wander alone, surround me with the grace of the Holy Spirit; when I am overcome, bring me help; call me back when I go astray; when I flee pull me back; break the hardness of my heart, enlighten me when I am blind, heal me when I am sick, and finally, you who raised Lazarus, raise me when I die. 15. Indeed, if you delay your help even a little, I will die. You who bring help, Father and source of all mercy, do not consider whom you help, but who you are. So do not delay, make haste, hurry and deliver me,[10] quickly, sweet Jesus, from the snare of my enemy[11] and from the jaws of this death. Amen.

II.

Shorter Version
July 10, 1338

Oh Jesus Christ,[12] oh my salvation, if human misery can arouse your mercy, rescue me, a wretched man, and favorably heed my prayers: grant me a journey according to your will and guide my steps on the way to eternal salvation; 2. deign to assist me on the day of my departure and in the final hour of my death, and do not remember my iniquities, but kindly receive the spirit that will come out of this poor body;[13] do not put your servant on trial, Lord. 3. O source of all mercy, treat me with mercy;[14] sustain my cause and cover my faults on the last day, and do not let this soul, the work of your hands, come under the haughty rule of my enemy and yours, or become prey to unclean spirits and source of ridicule for ravenous dogs, God my mercy.

III.

Almighty and eternal God, forgive those who fear you and spare those who implore you, so that the destructive forces of thunderstorms and the swirls of tempests are dispersed; may the threat of your majesty yield to the honor of your praise. For Christ our Lord. Amen.[15]

ORATIONES CONTRA TEMPESTATES AEREAS

IV.
Gloriosissime martirum Laurenti, qui, celesti fultus auxilio, ingestas corpori tuo flammas mirabiliter superasti, intercede, quesumus, apud eum a quo in illa victoria adiutus es, dominum nostrum Ihesum Christum, 2 ut ardores quoque presentium tempestatum per ipsius omnipotentiam nobis salvis misericorditer superentur. Amen.

V.
Dilecta Christo virgo Agatha, que ab eodem impetrare meruisti ut pestifer extuantis Ethne vapor a tuorum civium cervicibus arceretur, et nobis etiam, oramus, devotis tuis, impetra ut turbines ac vapores impendentium procellarum a nostris capitibus misericorditer avertantur. Per Christum dominum nostrum. Amen.

VI.
1. Miserator humani generis, Ihesu Christe, cui omnia famulantur, cuius in celo et in terra et in abysso par imperium est, infinitum et omnipotens, 2. consternatus animo et vehementer exterritus peccator ego quidem infelix et multorum michi delictorum conscius, sed tamen in te sperans, et in tribulationibus meis tuum nomen invocans, 3. misericordiam tuam supplex exoro ut me, ab ira tua liberatum, periculo repentine mortis eripias, 4. et has flammivomas nimborum minas, hanc ventorum rabiem, hos inquieti aeris tumultus omnipotentis dextere virtute compescas elementoque tuo iubeas quiescere. Per te, Ihesu Christe, salvator mundi.

VII.
1. Flos virginum, celi ac terre decus, sacra et ineffabilis virgo Maria, salvatoris nostri mater, a quo quicquid postulaveris facillime impetraturam esse confidimus, 2. te supplices deprecamur ut apud Christum, unicum et predulcem

PRAYERS AGAINST STORMS

IV.
O most glorious among the martyrs, Laurence,[16] who, sustained by heavenly aid, miraculously overcame the flames encircling your body, intercede, we pray, with the one by whom you were helped in that victory, our Lord Jesus Christ, so that we may escape unharmed the fires of the present storms,[17] mercifully saved, thanks to his omnipotence. Amen.[18]

V.
O Beloved to Christ, virgin Agatha,[19] who deserved to obtain from Him that the destructive fumes of the scorching Etna would be kept away from the heads of your fellow citizens, for us too, your followers, please, obtain that the whirlwinds and the cloud of the looming storms be mercifully turned away from our heads. For Christ our Lord. Amen.

VI.
With dismay in my soul and profoundly terrified, I implore you, who have mercy on mankind,[20] Jesus Christ, to whom all things are bound, whose kingdom is equally infinite and omnipotent in heaven, on earth, and in the abyss. 2. I, as an unhappy sinner and aware of my many faults, but nevertheless full of hope in you and ready to invoke your name in my tribulations, 3. in supplication I implore your mercy that you might save me from the danger of a sudden death, freed from your anger. 4. [I implore] that you might hold back, with the power of your almighty right hand, the flaring threats of the clouds, this rage of the winds, these disquieting tumults of the air, and command your elements to subside. For you, Jesus Christ, savior of the world.

VII.
O Flower of Virgins, adornment of heaven and earth, sacred and ineffable Virgin Mary, mother of our Savior, from whom we trust that you will obtain with great ease whatever you ask,[21] 2. we beseech and implore you to inter-

filium tuum, elementis et creaturis omnibus imperantem, pro nostra salute materne pietatis porrectis que ille suxit uberibus, 3. intercedas quatenus, longe fugatis tempestatibus atque ignibus horrificis, pluvia de nubibus salutaris hominibus, nec animantibus nec satis nocitura, nec arboribus, cum pace desiliat, 4. nobisque, tuis precibus a presenti metu et ab impremeditate ac rapide mortis discrimine liberatis, terris votiva quies, celo tranquilla redeat serenitas. Per eundem Christum dominum nostrum. Amen.

VIII.

1. Ihesu Christe piissime, cuius ubique potestas est, a cuius calore non est qui se abscondat, quoniam et si in celum adscendero tu illic es, et si descendero ad infernum ades; 2. qui posuisti terminos mari et terre et suis finibus consistere precepisti; qui imperas ventis et fluctibus: 3. te supplices in extremis casibus deprecamur ut pro salute nostra nunc imperium tuum omnipotenter exerceas, violentos ventorum impetus retundens, tumidos pelagi fluctus placans; 4. qui laborantem discipulorum naviculam, qui Petrum in fluctibus trepidantem a periculo liberasti, nos laborantes ac trepidos a vicine mortis periculo per misericordiam tuam libera; 5. tu nos creasti, tu creaturas tuas in tanta necessitate respice. 6. Non Eolum poscimus, non Nerea, non Tetidem, non Neptunum, sed te, unicum dominum ac salvatorem nostrum invocamus, Ihesum Christum, qui cum Deo patre et spiritu sancto vivis et regnas Deus per omnia secula.

IX.

1. Innumeris miraculis ac meritis fulgentes amici dei, N[icolae] atque H[erasme], quorum anime in celo triumphant, corpora in terris requiescunt, 2. qui, siti litoribus adversis, hic Barium possidens, hic Caietam, alter adriacas, alter thirrenas respicitis tempestates, quocunque tamen pelago iactatis, quacunque vasti maris parte laborantibus vocati, adesse et opem conferre consuevistis, 3. nunc adeste vocati pariter et metu ac lacrimosis precibus nostris moti, vos quibus navigantes fidunt, quibus tam multi incolumitatem

cede with Christ, your only and sweetest son, who commands the elements and all creatures. With that bosom of maternal tenderness offered for our salvation, from which he nourished himself, 3. do intercede so that, after the storms and the horrendous lightning have been driven away, from the clouds a peaceful rain may come that is healthy for men and not harmful to the animals, the crops, or the trees. 4. And to us, freed thanks to your prayers from the present fear and from the danger of an unexpected and violent death,[22] may longed-for peace return to earth, and quiet serenity in the sky. For our Lord Jesus Christ. Amen.

VIII.

O Most holy Jesus Christ, your power is everywhere, and no one can escape your fire, for even if I ascend to heaven you are there, and if I descend to hell you are there;[23] 2. you who have set the boundaries for the sea and for the earth, and you who order them to stay within their limits, you who command the winds and the waves:[24] 3. we beseech and implore you in these desperate instances to exercise omnipotently your command now for our salvation, repressing the violent impetus of the winds, placating the swollen waves of the sea; 4. you who freed from danger the boat of your disciples in distress, and Peter who trembled in the storm.[25] In your mercy, free us too, who are equally in distress and anxious about the imminent danger of death. 5. You created us; consider your creatures in such great need. 6. We do not implore Eolus, nor Nereus, nor Thetis, not Neptune, but we do implore you, our only Lord and Savior, Jesus Christ, who live and reign with God the Father and the Holy Spirit, God, for all ages.

IX.

O [help us] Friends of God, Nicholas and Erasmus,[26] resplendent for countless miracles and merits, whose souls triumph in heaven and whose bodies rest on earth,[27] 2. you who, buried on opposite shores, one in Bari, the other in Gaeta, look over the storms of the Adriatic and the Tyrrhenian Sea respectively, who, when called upon, have always helped and given hope to those who are tossed about in any sea, or to those who struggle in any part of the vast ocean.[28] 3. Now, invoked by us as well, help us, moved by our terror and

suam acceptam referunt, 4. ut nos quoque, vestra ope de tantis celi fretique motibus erepti, vestram presentiam sensibiliter cognoscamus; 5. pro nobis intercedite, quesumus, apud ipsum a quo vobis mirabilia posse datum est, dominum nostrum Ihesum Christum.

LA PREGHIERA NOTTURNA

X.
Noctu surgentis verba.
1. *In adventu.*
Heus, optime Ihesu Christe salvator, qui pro nostra salute in hunc mundum venisti et ad iudicium reversurus es, tibi rumpo horas noctis. Adesto, precor, et ad te venire cupientem suscipe, subleva, dirige, adiuva, rege, sustenta, et si parum cupio fac ut cupiam satis, in nomine patris et filii et spiritus sancti. Amen.

2. *In Natali usque ad purificationem.*
Heus, o Ihesu Christe salvator, qui pro nobis nasci dignatus es, tibi etc., adesto etc.

3. *Inde usque ad dominicam de passione.*
Heus, o Ihesu salvator, tibi etc.
Heus o Ihesu Christe salvator, qui pro nobis mori dignatus, tibi etc.

4. *Inde usque ad pascha exclusive.*
Redivive salvator, triumphator victorque mortis et inferni, tibi etc.
Salvator et celorum ascensor inclite, tibi etc.
Salvator missorque sancti spiritus parac1iti, tibi etc.

our tearful prayers, oh [help us] you, in whom sailors trust, by whom many say they were granted safety, 4. so that we too, rescued with your help from the great movements of the sky and the sea, may tangibly feel your presence. 5. We pray, intercede for us with the one from whom you have been granted the power to work miracles, our Lord Jesus Christ.

Night Prayer

X.
Words of those who rise at night
1. *In Advent*
Hear, Great Savior Jesus Christ, who came into this world for our salvation and will return on Judgment Day, for you I wake up in the hours of the night.[29] Assist me, I implore you, and receive me, for I desire to come to you; lift me, direct me, help me, support me, sustain me, and if my desire is feeble, make it strong enough. In the name of the Father, of the Son, and of the Holy Spirit. Amen.

2. *On Christmas day until the Feast of the Purification [of the Blessed Virgin Mary]*
Hear, Savior Jesus Christ, who have deigned to be born for us, for you . . . , etc., help us . . . , etc.

3. *From then [Purification] until Passion Sunday*
Hear, Savior Jesus Christ, for you . . . , etc.
Hear, Savior Jesus Christ, who have deigned to die for us, for you . . . , etc.

4. *From then exclusively until Easter*
Risen Savior, triumphant and victorious over death and hell, for you . . . , etc.
Glorious Savior, who ascended to heaven, for you . . . , etc.
O Savior and bearer of the Holy Spirit Paraclete, for you . . . , etc.

Notes

Autograph Prayers

1. This is the longest prayer, in prose, that Petrarch wrote on the first two folios of Paris Lat. 2201. The codex contains Cassiodorus's *De anima* and Augustine's *De vera religione*. The Augustinian influence is evident throughout the prayer. According to Rico, there is an unmistakable link between the voluntariness of sin and the Augustinian view of the imaginative life. Coppini sees the central notion of the desirable relationship of subjugation of the body to the soul, placed right at the beginning of the prayer and present throughout the following series of supplications, closely linked to Augustine's *De vera religione* (chs. 22–30 and 31). See Coppini, "Le preghiere del Petrarca," 598–99.

2. See psalm 2.10; Ez. 11.19 and 36.26.

3. See psalm 6.3; Jer. 17.14.

4. Ps. 118.149 (119.149); Job 7.9–10; psalm 5.5.

5. Ps. 12.4 (13.3); 118.35 (119.35); 118.133 (119.133); 26.9 (27.9); 142.7 (143.7); and Lk 1.79. See also psalm 4.17.

6. Ps. 50.12 (51.11).

7. See Aquinas (?) *Adoro te devote* 15–16: "Fac me tibi semper magis credere, in te spem habere, te diligere" (Make me always believe in you, have hope in you, love you); Deut. 6.5: "Diliges Dominum Deum tuum ex toto corde tuo et ex tota anima tua et ex tota fortitudine tua" (You shall love the Lord your God with all your heart and with all your soul and with all your might); New Testament: Lk. 10.27; Mk. 13.30; Mt. 22.37.

8. "Salvum me fac" is a recurring invocation in the Psalms.

9. See psalm 4.19.

10. See psalm 5.10; Eusebius of Cremona, *De mortis Sancti Hieronymi* (PL 22.269): "Surge, propera—Inclina ad me aurem tuum, accelera, ut de hac lacrymarum valle eripias me" (Arise, hasten—Incline your ear to me, hasten to rescue me from this vale of tears).

11. See psalm 1.18. On the snare metaphor in Petrarch and the Bible, see psalm 1 n. 21.

12. Known as the *brevior*, this abridgment of the previous longer prayer is the most reproduced in the manuscript tradition. Under the title *Oratio quotidiana*, it is often placed, alone or with other Petrarchan prayers, after Petrarch's psalms, even in the codex of Luzern (Zentralbibliothek, S 20 4°), a reliable witness of Petrarch's psalms, where it is perfectly identical to the autograph of Paris Lat. 2201. As Coppini notes, this may suggest that this order was most likely according

to Petrarch's wishes and could be considered as evidence for backdating the psalms to the year 1338 instead of the traditionally accepted date of 1347–48. See Coppini, "Le preghiere del Petrarca," 599. On the dating of Petrarch's psalms, see introduction note 25.

13. *Corpusculo*: this recurring expression in Petrarch for the fleetingness of the human body is present in Juvenal 10.173: "mors sola fatetur / quantula sint hominum corpuscula" (death alone shows how insignificant are the fragile bodies of human beings). Cited also in the *Secretum* 2.11.

14. Ps. 50.3 (51.2): "Miserere mei Deus secundum misericordiam tuam iuxta multitudinem miserationum tuarum dele iniquitates meas" (Have mercy on me, O God, according to your steadfast love; according to your abundant mercy, blot out my transgressions); and 137.8 (138.8). See also Petrarch's psalm 3.7.

15. This is the only *oratio contra tempestates aereas* in MS Paris Lat. 2201 and the only one in this category in Petrarch's hand. See also *Corpus orationum*, 14 vols., ed. Edmond Eugène Moeller et al. (Turnhout: Brepols, 1992), 6:3875a and 6:3875b.

Prayers against Storms

16. Laurence is the name of the archdeacon of the Church of Rome martyred in Rome in 258 during the persecution of Christians ordered by Emperor Valerian. According to Ambrose, he was burned alive on a grill, the instrument with which he is iconographically represented. Devotion to the saint developed rapidly and beyond Rome. His steadfast courage in the face of death is mentioned by Dante in the fourth canto of *Paradiso*. He is also the subject of Frate Cipolla's fantastic preaching in the tenth story on the sixth day, in Boccaccio's *Decameron*.

17. In the Missal on the feast day of St. Laurence (August 10) the prayer of intercession to the saint creates a parallel between the flames burning his body and the flames of sin: "Da nobis, quǽsumus, omnípotens Deus: vitiórum nostrórum flammas exstínguere; qui beáto Lauréntio tribuísti tormentórum suórum incéndia superáre" (Grant us, we pray, almighty God, to extinguish the flames of our sins, just as you granted Saint Laurence to overcome the fires of his tortures). See *Corpus orationum*, 2:960.

18. The first four prayers against storms (here 4–7), first published by Attilio Hortis in 1874 and based on the codice Laurenziano 90, were later published by Rauner together with Petrarch's psalms and other prayers on the basis of a greater number of witnesses, which attribute them all to Petrarch. The prayers are respectively addressed to St. Laurence, Agatha, Christ, and the Virgin Mary. At times

they appear along with the *orationes quotidiana* and two other prayers *contra tempestates*, one to Christ and the other to two saints (here nos. 8 and 9). Petrarch's notorious terror of sea storms and sea voyages was the main reason for his refusal to undertake a pilgrimage to the Holy Land expressed in the preface of the *Itinerarium*, where, paradoxically, Petrarch appears more troubled by the prospect of seasickness than of death: "Longam mortem et peiorem morte nauseam, non de nichilo quidem sed expertus, metuo" (I fear slow death and nausea worse than death itself, not without reason but from experience). See Cachey, *Petrarch's Guide to the Holy Land*, fol. 2r. On Petrarch's fear of the sea and shipwreck, see psalm 1; and for relevant bibliography, notes 12 and 13 and psalm 6.

19. Agatha (feast day, February 5), a legendary saint and martyr in Catania under Decius or Diocletian. From at least late antiquity into the modern era, she was invoked as protector against disasters caused by fire and in particular against eruptions of Etna and earthquakes in general.

20. *Miserator . . . famulantur* recalls *Corpus orationum*, 6:3807: "Omnipotens sempiterne Deus, cui cuncta famulantur elementa" (Almighty and everlasting God, to whom all the elements serve).

21. *Fam.* 12.15.7: "Facile tamen ab humanitate tua me impetraturum spero" (I nevertheless hope to accomplish it easily because of your kindness); *Le familiari*, 3:42; *Letters on Familiar Matters*, 2:165.

22. As Coppini notes, this fear of "impremeditate ac rapide mortis" (unexpected and violent death) is the same fear of the "vicine mortis periculo" (imminent danger of death) of the following prayer to Christ (no. 8) and of the "vicine mortis metus" (fear of imminent death) of *Fam.* 5.5.7.

23. *Si . . . ades* recalls Ps. 138.8 (139.8), cited in Augustine's *Confessions* 1.2.2 and in *Dvs*.1.5.12.

24. Ps. 103.6–9 (104.6–9); Lk. 8.25: "quis putas hic est quia et ventis imperat et mari et oboediunt ei" (Who then is this, that he commands even the winds and the water and they obey him?).

25. Mk. 4.37–39; Lk. 8.22–24; Mt. 14.28–32.

26. The saints indicated with only initials in the codices (and left as such in Hortis and Rauner's editions) have been identified by Coppini as St. Nicholas and St. Erasmus, both known as patron saints of sailors. Venerated in Bari, Nicholas is traditionally associated with the sea and maritime trade and navigation. Among his best-known miracles are those of calming storms at sea. St. Erasmo (or Elmo) was also known as protector of sailors. According to tradition, he was miraculously transported to Formia during the persecution of Emperor Diocletian. However, he is most certainly a saint originally from Formia. A borough of the city of Gaeta, a few miles away, is named after him.

27. *Corpus orationum*, 2:1463: "Deus, qui beatum Nicolaum, pontificem tuum, innumeris decorasti miraculis" (God, you have adorned blessed Nicholas, your pontiff, with innumerable miracles).

28. *Fam.* 9.13.33: "sicut Adriatici fremitum maris vidit, sic thirrenas aspiciat tempestates" (just as he saw the roaring of the Adriatic, he will witness the Tyrrhenian tempests); *Le familiari*, 2:254; *Letters on Familiar Matters*, 2:41.

Night Prayer

29. Petrarch's nocturnal prayer presents variations according to the different liturgical seasons. Since the one to be recited in Advent is written in full, we could assume that it was written during that season. Together with Lent, Advent is considered a "strong" liturgical season. The *etc.* in the following prayers indicates the repetition of words from the Advent prayer: *tibi etc.* means "tibi rumpo horas noctis," and *adesto etc.* suggests that all the words that follow *adesto* in the Advent prayer (i.e., from *adesto* to the end) are to be repeated. Petrarch refers to his habit of getting up at night for the night office in *Sen.* 10.2.5: "Quotiens per estate media nocte surrexerim et, nocturnis Christo laudibus persolutis unus ego, ne somno pressos famulos inquietarem, nunc in agros presertim sublustri luna, nunc in montes exierim?" (How often would I rise in the middle of the night throughout the summer, and, after reciting alone the nightly office in praise of Christ, go out at times into the fields, especially in the moonlight, and at times into the mountains—all alone, not to disturb the servants who were sound asleep?). *Res seniles*, 3:162; *Letters of Old Age*, 2:365.

BIBLIOGRAPHY

Primary Sources

Alighieri, Dante. *Convivio*. In *The Princeton Dante Project*. https://dante.princeton.edu/.

———. *Paradiso*. Ed. and trans. Robert Hollander. New York: Doubleday, 2007.

Ambrose. *Hexaemeron*. In CC. https://mlat.uzh.ch/.

Augustine of Hippo. *The City of God*. In *The Works of Saint Augustine: A Translation for the 21st Century*, introd. and trans. William Babcock. Hyde Park, NY: New City Press, 1990.

———. *De civitate dei*. In CC. https://mlat.uzh.ch/.

———. *The Confessions*. Ed. John E. Rotelle, trans. and introd. Maria Boulding. Hyde Park, NY: New City Press, 1997.

———. *De doctrina christiana*. In CC. https://mlat.uzh.ch/.

———. *Expositions of the Psalms 33–50*. In *The Works of Saint Augustine: A Translation for the 21st Century*. Hyde Park, NY: New City Press, 1990.

———. *Expositions of the Psalms 121–150*. In *The Works of Saint Augustine: A Translation for the 21st Century*, ed. Edmund Hill, John E. Rotelle, and Allan D. Fitzgerald. Brooklyn, NY: New City Press, 1990.

———. *In Evangelium Iohannis tractatus*. Corpus Christianorum Series Latina, vol. 36. Turnhout: Brepols, 1954.

———. *Sermons 184–229Z*. In *The Works of Saint Augustine: A Translation for the 21st Century*. New Rochelle, NY: New City Press, 1990.

———. *Sermons 230–272B*. In *The Works of Saint Augustine: A Translation for the 21st Century*. New Rochelle, NY: New City Press, 1990.

———. *Soliloquia*. In CC. https://mlat.uzh.ch/.

———. *Soliloquies: Augustine's Inner Dialogue*. Ed. John E. Rotelle, trans. Kim Paffenroth, and introd. Boniface Ramsey. Hyde Park, NY: New City Press, 2000.

Aquinas, Thomas. *Adoro te devote*. https://hymnary.org/.

———. *Summa theologiae*. In *Opera omnia S. Thomae*. Online Corpus Thomisticum project, University of Navarre. http://www.corpusthomisticum.org/.
Cassian. *Institutiones*. In CC. https://mlat.uzh.ch/.
Cassiodorus. *Expositio psalmorum*. In CC. https://mlat.uzh.ch/.
———. *De anima*. In CC. https://mlat.uzh.ch/.
Cicero. *De natura deorum*. Ed. Arthur Stanley Pease. Cambridge, MA: Harvard University Press, 1955.
———. *Pro Roscio Amerino*. In CC. https://mlat.uzh.ch/.
———. *Tusculanus*. In CC. https://mlat.uzh.ch/.
Corpus orationum. Ed. Edmond Eugène Moeller, Jean-Marie Clément, Bertrandus Coppieters 't Wallant, and Louis-Marie Couillaud. Turnhout: Brepols, 1992.
Eusebius of Cremona. *De mortis Sancti Hieronymi*. PL 22.269.
Francis of Assisi. *Francis of Assisi: Early Documents*. 3 vols. Ed. Regis J. Armstrong et al. Hyde Park, NY: New City Press, 1999.
———. *Scritti*. Ed. Aristide Cabassi. Padua: Edizioni francescane, 2002.
Gregory the Great. *Moralia in Iob*. In CC. https://mlat.uzh.ch/.
Horace. *Odes*. In CC. https://mlat.uzh.ch/.
Jerome. *Epistola ad Eustochium* (22). In CC. https://mlat.uzh.ch/.
Lactantius. *Divinae Institutiones*. In CC. https://mlat.uzh.ch/.
Matthieu de Vendôme. *Tobias*. In *Mathei Vindocinensis opera*, ed. Franco Munari. Rome: Edizioni di Storia e Letteratura, 1977.
Ovid. *Amores*. In CC. https://mlat.uzh.ch/.
———. *Metamorphoses*. In CC. https://mlat.uzh.ch/.
———. *Metamorphoses*. Ed. Arthur Golding and Madeleine Forey. Baltimore: Johns Hopkins University Press, 2002.
Petrarca, Francesco. *L'Africa: Edizione critica per cura di Nicola Festa; corredata di un ritratto e cinque tavole fuori testo*. Florence: Sansoni, 1926.
———. *De otio religioso*. Ed. Giulio Goletti. Florence: Le Lettere, 2006.
———. *De vita solitaria*. Ed. Guido Martellotti. Turin: Einaudi, 1977.
———. *Epistulae Metricae / Briefe in Versen*. Ed. Otto Schönberger and Eva Schönberger. Würzburg: Königshausen & Neumann, 2004.
———. *Le familiari*. 4 vols. Ed. Vittorio Rossi. Florence: Sansoni, 1968.
———. *Francesco Petrarca, Invectives*. Ed. David Marsh. Cambridge, MA: Harvard University Press, 2003.
———. *Lettere disperse*. Ed. Alessandro Pancheri. Milan-Parma: Fondazione Pietro Bembo-U. Guanda, 1994.
———. *Letters of Old Age. Rerum senilium libri*. 2 vols. Ed. and trans. Aldo S. Bernardo, Saul Levin, and Reta A. Bernardo. Baltimore: Johns Hopkins University Press, 1992.

———. *Letters on Familiar Matters: Rerum familiarum libri*. 3 vols. Ed. and trans. Aldo S. Bernardo. Albany: State University of New York Press, 1975; repr. Baltimore: Johns Hopkins University Press, 1982–85.

———. *Liber sine nomine*. Trans. Laura Casarsa. Turin: Aragno, 2010.

———. *My Secret Book*. Ed. and trans. Nicholas Mann. Cambridge, MA: Harvard University Press, 2016.

———. *Petrarch on Religious Leisure*. Ed. and trans. Susan S. Schearer. New York: Italica, 2002.

———. *Petrarch's Africa*. Trans. and annot. Thomas G. Bergin and Alice Wilson. New Haven, CT: Yale University Press, 1977.

———. *Petrarch's Bucolicum Carmen*. Ed. and trans. Thomas G. Bergin. New Haven, CT: Yale University Press, 1974.

———. *Petrarch's Lyric Poems: The Rime Sparse and Other Lyrics*. Ed. Robert M. Durling. Cambridge, MA: Harvard University Press, 1976.

———. *Petrarch's Remedies for Fortune Fair and Foul*. 5 vols. Ed., trans., and comm. C. H. Rawski. Bloomington: Indiana University Press, 1991.

———. *Pétrarque: Les Psaumes Pénitentiaux publiés d'après le manuscrit de la Bibliothèque de Lucerne; préf. de Pierre de Nolhac*. Ed. Henri Cochin. Paris: L. Rouart, 1929.

———. *Pétrarque: Les remèdes aux deux fortunes*. 2 vols. Ed. and trans. Christophe Carraud. Grenoble: Millon, 2002.

———. *Psalmi penitentiales; Orationes*. Ed. Donatella Coppini. Florence: Le Lettere, 2010.

———. *Rerum memorandarum libri*. Ed. Marco Petoletti. Florence: Le Lettere, 2014.

———. *Rerum vulgarium fragmenta; Canzoniere*. Ed. Marco Santagata. Milan: Mondadori, 1996.

———. *Secretum. De secretu conflictu curarum mearum; Il mio segreto*. Ed. Enrico Fenzi. Milan: Mursia, 1992.

———. *Seniles. Rerum senilium libri; Le senili*. 4 vols. Ed. Silvia Rizzo and Monica Berté. Florence: Le Lettere, 2017.

Plautus. *Epidicus*. In CC. https://mlat.uzh.ch/.

Pliny the Elder. *Naturalis Historiae*. In CC. https://mlat.uzh.ch/.

Saint-Victor, William (of). *Sermo*. In CC. https://mlat.uzh.ch/.

Sallustius. *Bellum Iugurthinum*. In CC. https://mlat.uzh.ch/.

Sedulius. *Sedulii Scotti collectaneum miscellaneum*. Ed. Dean Simpson and François Dolbeau. Turnhout: Brepols, 1988.

Seneca. *Ad Lucilium Epistulae Morales*. In CC. https://mlat.uzh.ch/.

———. *De Beneficiis*. In CC. https://mlat.uzh.ch/.

———. *De iram*. In CC. https://mlat.uzh.ch/.
———. *De Tranquillitate*. In CC. https://mlat.uzh.ch/.
———. *Hercules furens*. In CC. https://mlat.uzh.ch/.
Springer, Carl P. E., ed. *Sedulius, The Paschal Song and Hymns*. Atlanta, GA: SBL Press, 2013.
Statius. *Thebaid*. In CC. https://mlat.uzh.ch/.
Terence. *Adelphoe*. In CC. https://mlat.uzh.ch/.
Virgil. *Aeneid*. In CC. https://mlat.uzh.ch/.

SECONDARY SOURCES

Ardissino, Erminia. *Poesia in forma di preghiera: Svelamenti dell'essere da Francesco d'Assisi ad Alda Merini*. Rome: Carocci, 2023.
Ariani, Marco. *Petrarca*. Rome: Salerno, 1999.
Ascoli, Albert R. "Blinding the Cyclops." In *Petrarch and Dante: Anti-Dantism, Metaphysics, Tradition*, ed. Zygmunt Barański and Theodore J. Cachey Jr., 114–73. Notre Dame, IN: University of Notre Dame Press, 2009.
Ayo, Nicholas, C.S.C. *Gloria Patri*. Notre Dame, IN: University of Notre Dame Press, 2007.
Baglio, Marco. "Presenze dantesche nel Petrarca latino." *Studi petrarcheschi* 9 (1992): 77–136.
Baltzer, Rebecca A., and Margot Fassler, eds. *The Divine Office in the Latin Middle Ages Methodology and Source Studies, Regional Developments, Hagiography: Written in Honor of Professor Ruth Steiner*. Oxford: Oxford University Press, 2000.
Barański, Zygmunt. "'Io mi rivolgo indietro a ciascun passo' (*Rvf*. 15. 1): Petrarch, the Fabula of Eurydice and Orpheus, and the Structure of the *Canzoniere*." In *Dante, Petrarch, Boccaccio: Literature, Doctrine, Reality*, ed. Zygmunt Barański, 393–416. Cambridge: Legenda, 2020.
Barney, Stephen A. *The Etymologies of Isidore of Seville*. Cambridge: Cambridge University Press, 2006.
Billanovich, Giuseppe. "Dalle prime alle ultime letture del Petrarca." In *Il Petrarca ad Arquà: Atti del Convegno di studi nel VI centenario (1370–1374) (Arquà Petrarca, 6–8 nov. 1970). Annali della Scuola Normale Superiore di Pisa. Classe di Lettere e Filosofia*, ed. L. Goggi Carotti, 13–50. Padua: Antenore, 1975.
———. "Nella biblioteca del Petrarca; Il Petrarca, il Boccaccio e le 'Enarrationes in Psalmos' di S. Agostino." *Italia medioevale e umanistica* 3 (1960): 1–58.

Boccuti, Mattia. "L'umile salmista e il poeta laureato." *Italica* 98.2 (2021): 254–66.

Brovia, Romana. "'Vacate et Videte' il modello della 'lectio divina' nel 'De otio religioso.'" *Petrarchesca* 1 (2013): 77–91.

Cachey, Theodore J., Jr. "From Shipwreck to Port: *Rvf* 189 and the Making of the *Canzoniere.*" *MLN* 120 (2005): 30–49.

———. "*Peregrinus* (quasi) ubique: Petrarca e la storia del viaggio." *Intersezioni* 17.3 (1997): 369–84.

———. *Petrarch's Guide to the Holy Land.* Notre Dame, IN: University of Notre Dame Press, 2002.

Camerino, Giuseppe Antonio. "'Per aspro mare': In margine a R.V.F. CLXXXIX." *Italianistica* 21.2–3 (1992): 503–9.

Casali, Marino. "Imitazione e ispirazione nei 'Salmi penitenziali' del Petrarca." *Studi petrarcheschi* 7 (1961): 151–70.

———. "Per una più precisa datazione dei 'Salmi Penitenziali' del Petrarca." *Humanitas* 10 (1955): 696–704.

———. "Petrarca 'Penitenziale': Dai Salmi alle Rime." *Lettere italiane* 20.3 (1968): 366–82.

Cassian. *Conference Ten on Prayer.* New York: Paulist Press, 1985.

Chapman, George. *Seven Penitentiall Psalmes paraphrastically translated: with other philosophicall poems, and a hymne to Christ vpon the crosse.* London: Imprinted [by R. Field] for Matthevv Selman, 1612.

Constable, Giles. "Petrarch and Monasticism." In *Francesco Petrarca, Citizen of the World: Proceedings of the World Petrarch Congress, Washington, D.C., April 6–13, 1974,* ed. Aldo S. Bernardo, 53–99. Padua: Antenore, 1980.

Contini, Gianfranco. "Un'ipotesi sulle *Laudes creaturarum.*" In *Varianti e altra linguistica,* ed. Gianfranco Contini, 141–59. Turin: Einaudi, 1970.

Coppini, Donatella. "Adonay domine deus: Preghiere attribuite a Petrarca nella tradizione manoscritta." *Quaderni petrarcheschi* 17–18 (2007–8): 1139–60.

———. "Petrarca, i salmi e il codice parigino latino 1994 delle 'Enarrationes' di Agostino." In *Petrarca e Agostino,* ed. Roberto Cardini and Donatella Coppini, 19–38. Rome: Bulzoni, 2004.

———. "Preghiere." In *Petrarca nel tempo: Tradizione lettori e immagini delle opere. Catalogo della mostra, Arezzo, Sottochiesa di San Francesco, 22 novembre 2003–27 gennaio 2004,* ed. Michele Feo, 446–54. Pisa: Bandecchi & Vivaldi, 2003.

———. "Le preghiere del Petrarca." In *Estravaganti, Disperse, Apocrifi Petrarcheschi,* ed. Claudia Barra and Paola Vecchi Galli, 595–612. Milan: Cisalpino, 2006.

Costley King'oo, Clare. *Miserere Mei*. Notre Dame, IN: University of Notre Dame Press, 2012.

Crevatin, Giuliana. "L'ultimo viaggio di Ariovisto: Un percorso intertestuale." In *Studi offerti a Luigi Blasucci*, ed. Lucio Lugnani, Marco Santagata, and Alfredo Stussi, 223–30. Lucca: Pacini, 1996.

Crichton, J. D. "The Office in the West: The Early Middle-Ages." In *The Study of Liturgy*, ed. C. James, G. Wainwright, and E. Yarnald. Oxford: Oxford University Press, 1978.

Delisle, M. Léopold. "Notice sur un livre annoté par Pétrarque (ms. latin 2201 de la Bibliothèque Nationale)." In *Notices et extraits des manuscrits de la Bibliothèque Nationale et autres bibliothèques*, tome 35, parte II, 393–408. Paris: Klincksieck, 1897.

de Nolhac, Pierre. *Pétrarque et l'humanisme*. 2 vols. Paris: Champion, 1907.

Dotti, Ugo. *Vita di Petrarca*. Turin: Aragno, 2014.

Driscoll, Michael S. "The Seven Penitential Psalms: Their Designation and Usages from the Middle Ages Onwards." *Ecclesia Orans* 17 (2000): 153–201.

Dyer, Joseph. "The Singing of Psalms in the Early-Medieval Office." *Speculum* 64.3 (1989): 535–78.

Feo, Michele, ed. *Codici latini del Petrarca nelle biblioteche fiorentine*. Florence: Le Lettere, 1991.

———. *Guido Martellotti: Scritti petrarcheschi*. Padua: Antenore, 1983.

Fera, Vincenzo. "Petrarca e la poetica dell'incultum." *Studi medievali e umanistici* 10 ([2012] 2015): 9–87.

———. "Testo e gestualità: Un versetto penitenziale del Petrarca." *Quaderni Veneti* 2 (2013): 119–28.

Fontaine, Jacques. *Naissance de la poésie dans l'occident chrétien. Esquisse d'une histoire de la poésie latine chrétienne du IIIe au VIe siècle. Avec une préface de Jacques Perret*. Paris: Études Augustiniennes, 1981.

Fulton Brown, Rachel. "Exegesis, Mimesis, and the Voice of Christ in Francis of Assisi's *Office of the Passion*." *Medieval Journal* 4.2 (2014): 39–62.

Fumagalli, Edoardo. "Petrarca e la Bibbia." In *La Bibbia nella letteratura italiana: Dal Medioevo al Rinascimento*, ed. Pietro Gibellini, 5:271–304. Brescia: Morcelliana, 2009.

Geri, Lorenzo, and Ester Pietrobon, eds. *Lirica e sacro tra Medioevo e Rinascimento (secoli XIII–XVI)*. Canterano (RM): Aracne editrice, 2020.

———. "Varia fortuna del Petrarca 'monastico.'" In *Petrarca, l'Italia, l'Europa: Sulla varia fortuna di Petrarca. Bari, 20–22 maggio 2015*, ed. Davide Canfora, 171–82. Bari: Edizioni di Pagina, 2016.

Gerosa, Pietro Paolo. *Umanesimo cristiano del Petrarca*. Turin: Bottega d'Erasmo, 1966.

Giannarelli, Elena. "Quale e quanto Agostino ai tempi del Petrarca." In *Petrarca e Agostino*, ed. Roberto Cardini, and Donatella Coppini, 1–18. Rome: Bulzoni, 2004.

Gigliucci, Roberto. *Oxymoron Amoris*. Anzio: De Rubeis, 1990.

———. *Salmi penitenziali*. Rome: Salerno, 1997.

———. *Lo spettacolo della morte*. Anzio: De Rubeis, 1944.

Goins, Scott. "Jerome Psalters." In *The Oxford Handbook of the Psalms*, ed. William P. Brown, 185–98. Oxford: Oxford University Press, 2014.

Goletti, Giulio. "Il breviario del Petrarca." In *Petrarca nel tempo: Tradizione lettori e immagini delle opere. Catalogo della mostra, Arezzo, Sottochiesa di San Francesco, 22 novembre 2003–27 gennaio 2004*, ed. Michele Feo, 513–15. Pontedera: Bandecchi & Vivaldi, 2003.

———. "*Scriptura qua utimur*: La Bibbia del Petrarca." *Quaderni petrarcheschi* 17–18 (2005–6): 629–77.

———. "'Volentes unum aliud agimus': La questione del dissidio interiore e il cristianesimo petrarchesco." *Quaderni petrarcheschi* 7 (1990): 65–108.

Graves, Michael. *Jerome, Epistle 106 (on the Psalms)*. Atlanta, GA: SBL Press, 2022.

———. *Jerome's Hebrew Philology: A Study Based on His Commentary on Jeremiah*. Leiden: Brill, 2007.

Greene, Thomas M. *The Vulnerable Text: Essays on Renaissance Literature*. New York: Columbia University Press, 1986.

Heffernan, Thomas, and E. Ann Matter, eds. *The Liturgy of the Medieval Church*. Kalamazoo: Medieval Institute Publications, Western Michigan University, 2001.

Hornby, Emma. "Pia dictamina." In *The Canterbury Dictionary of Hymnology*. Canterbury Press. https://hymnology.hymnsam.co.uk/.

Janson, Tore. *Prose Rhythm in Medieval Latin from the 9th to the 13th Century*. Stockholm: Almqvist & Wiksell International, 1975.

Kircher, Timothy. *The Poet's Wisdom: The Humanists, the Church, and the Formation of Philosophy in the Early Renaissance*. Leiden: Brill, 2005.

Leclercq, Jean. "Temi monastici nell'opera del Petrarca." *Lettere italiane* 43 (1991): 42–54.

Leonardi, Lino, Caterina Menichetti, and Sara Natale, eds. *Le traduzioni italiane della Bibbia nel Medioevo: Catalogo dei manoscritti (secoli XIII–XV)*. Florence: Edizioni del Galluzzo, 2018.

Lindsay, Wallace Martin. *Isidori Hispalensis Episcopi: Etymologiarvm sive originvm.* Vol. 1, *Libros I–X.* Oxford: Oxford University Press, 2016.

Lokaj, Rodney J. "Petrarca-alter Franciscus, ovvero un'ascesa francescana del Monte Ventoso." *Il Veltro. Rivista della Civiltà Italiana* 5–6 (1998): 465–79.

———. "San Francesco in Petrarca ovvero, verso una semiologia francescana in Petrarca." In *San Francesco e il francescanesimo nella letteratura italiana dal XIII al XV secolo, Atti del Convegno Nazionale (Assisi, 10–12 dicembre 1999),* ed. Stanislao Da Campagnola and Pasquale Tuscano, 169–94. Assisi: Accademia Properziana del Subasio, 2001.

Luciani, Evelyine. *Les Confessions de Saint Augustin dans les lettres de Petrarque.* Paris: Études Augustiniennes, 1982.

Luibhéid, Colm, and Eugène Pichery, eds. *John Cassian Conferences.* New York: Paulist Press, 1985.

Lummus, David G. *City of Poetry: Imagining the Civic Role of the Poet in Fourteenth-Century Italy.* Cambridge: Cambridge University Press, 2020.

Maggi, Armando, and Victoria Kirkham, eds. *Petrarch: A Critical Guide to the Complete Works.* Chicago: University of Chicago Press, 2009.

Maldina, Nicolò. "Penitenza ed elegia nel *Canzoniere* del Petrarca." In *La Bibbia in poesia*, ed. Rosanna Pettinelli, 17–33. Rome: Bulzoni, 2015.

———. "Petrarca e il libro dei 'Salmi': Materiali per la struttura dei 'Rerum Vulgarium Fragmenta.'" *Lettere italiane* 66.4 (2014): 543–58.

Mantello, F. A. C., and A. G. Rigg, eds. *Medieval Latin: An Introduction and Bibliographical Guide.* Washington, DC: Catholic University of America Press, 1966.

Mariani, Ugo. *Il Petrarca e gli Agostiniani.* Rome: Edizoni di Storia e Letteratura, 1946.

Martellotti, Guido. "Clausole e ritmi nella prosa narrativa del Petrarca." In *Guido Martellotti: Scritti petrarcheschi*, ed. Michele Feo and Silvia Rizzo, 207–19. Padua: Antenore, 1983.

Martinelli, Bortolo. *Il "Secretum" conteso.* Naples: Loffredo, 1982.

Martinez, Ronald. "Places and Times of the Liturgy from Dante to Petrarch." In *Petrarch and Dante*, ed. Zygmunt Barański and Theodore J. Cachey Jr., 320–70. Notre Dame, IN: University of Notre Dame Press, 2009.

Matter, E. Ann. "Petrarch's Personal Psalms (*Psalmi penitentiales*)." In *Petrarch: A Critical Guide to the Complete Works*, ed. Armando Maggi and Victoria Kirkham, 219–27. Chicago: University of Chicago Press, 2009.

Mazzotta, Giuseppe. *The Worlds of Petrarch.* Durham, NC: Duke University Press, 1993.

Mitchell, Nathan D. "*Ordo Psallendi* in the *Rule*: Historical Perspectives." *American Benedictine Review* 20 (1969): 505–18.
Mommsen, Theodore E., ed. *Petrarch's Testament*. Ithaca, NY: Cornell University Press, 1957.
Niccoli, Alessandro. "Musaico." In *Enciclopedia dantesca*. https://www.treccani.it/enciclopedia/musaico_%28Enciclopedia-Dantesca%29/.
Oberhelman, S. M. "The History and Development of the *Cursus Mixtus* in Latin Literature." *Classical Quarterly* 38.1 (1988): 228–42.
Ossa-Richardson, Anthony, and Margaret Meserve, eds. *Et Amicorum: Essays on Renaissance Humanism and Philosophy in Honour of Jill Kraye*. Leiden: Brill, 2018.
Picone, Michelangelo. *Il Canzoniere: Lettura micro e macrotestuale*. Ravenna: Longo, 2007.
———. "Il motivo della 'navigatio' nel *Canzoniere* del Petrarca." *Atti e Memorie della Accademia Petrarca di Lettere, Arti e Scienze* 51 (1989): 291–307.
Pierce, Joanne M. *Medieval Christian Liturgy*. https://doi.org/10.1093/acrefore/9780199340378.013.84.
Pietrobon, Ester. "Fare penitenza all'ombra di Dante: Questioni di poesia e devozione nei *Sette salmi*." *L'Alighieri* 51 (2018): 63–80.
———. *La penna interprete della cetra: I "Salmi" in volgare e la poesia spirituale italiana nel Rinascimento*. Rome: Edizioni di Storia e Letteratura, 2019.
———. "*Tam efficaciter utinam quam inculte*: Modelli liturgici e stile monastico nei *Psalmi penitentiales*." *Petrarchesca* 7 (2019): 47–65.
Pintacuda, Paolo. "Una traduzione spagnola dei *Salmi penitenziali* petrarcheschi: Studio ed edizione." In *Francesco Petrarca l'opera latina: Tradizione e fortuna*, ed. Luisa Secchi Tarugi, 391–418. Florence: Franco Cesati, 2004.
Pozzi, Giovanni. "Petrarca, i padri e soprattutto la Bibbia." *Studi petrarcheschi* 6 (1989): 125–69.
Quigley, Edward J. *The Divine Office: A Study of the Roman Breviary*. Project Gutenberg (open access). https://www.gutenberg.org/.
Regn, Gerhard, and Bernhard Huss. "Petrarch's Rome: The History of the *Africa* and the Renaissance Project." *MLN* 124.1 (2009): 86–102.
Rico, Francisco. *Vida u obra de Petrarca*: Vol. 1: *Lectura del Secretum*. Barcelona: Ariel, 1974.
Roberts, Michael. *Biblical Epic and Rhetorical Paraphrase in Late Antiquity*. Liverpool: Francis Cairns, 1985.
Ryrie, Alec, and Jessica Martin, eds. *Private and Domestic Devotion in Early Modern Britain*. Farnham: Ashgate, 2012.

Saenger, Paul. "Books of Hours and the Reading Habits of the Later Middle Ages." In *The Culture of Print: Power and the Uses of Print in Early Modern Europe*, ed. Roger Chartier and trans. Lydia G. Cochrane, 141–73. Princeton, NJ: Princeton University Press, 2016.

———. "Silent Reading: Its Impact on Late Medieval Script and Society." *Viator* 13 (1982): 367–414.

———. *Space between Words: The Origins of Silent Reading*. Stanford: Stanford University Press, 1997.

Santagata, Marco. *Per le moderne carte*. Bologna: Il Mulino, 1990.

Santini, Carlo. "Nuovi accertamenti sull'ipotesi di raffronto tra Silvio e Petrarca." In *Preveggenze umanistiche di Petrarca: Atti delle giornate petrarchesche di Tor Vergata (Roma/Cortona 1–2 giugno 1992)*, ed. Francesco Tateo, 111–39. Pisa: ETS, 1993.

Scotto, Dominic F., TOR. "St. Francis and the Spirit of the Liturgy." *The Cord* 32.1 (1982):13–17.

Serjeantson, Deirdre. "The Book of Psalms and the Early Modern Sonnet." *Renaissance Studies* 29.4 (2015): 632–49.

Springer, Carl P. E. *The Gospel as Epic in Late Antiquity: The Paschale Carmen of Sedulius*. Leiden: Brill, 1988.

Stuart, Duane Reed. "Petrarch's Indebtedness to the *Libellus* of Catullus." *Transactions and Proceedings of the American Philological Association* 48 (1917): 3–26.

Szövérffy, Joseph. *A Concise History of Medieval Latin Hymnody*. Leyden: Classical Folia Editions, 1985.

Taft, Robert. *The Liturgy of the Hours in East and West*. Collegeville, MN: Liturgical Press, 1986.

Traill, David A. *Carmina Burana*. Cambridge, MA: Harvard University Press, 2018.

Van Deusen, Nancy. *The Place of the Psalms in Intellectual Culture of the Middle Ages*. Albany: State University of New York Press, 1999.

Van Dijk, S. J. P. *Origins of the Modern Roman Liturgy: The Liturgy of the Papal Court and the Franciscan Order in the Thirteenth Century*. Westminster: Newman Press, 1960.

Velli, Giuseppe. "Petrarca e i poeti cristiani." *Studi petrarcheschi* 6 (1989): 171–78.

———. "Petrarca e la grande poesia latina del XII secolo." *Italia medioevale e umanistica* 28 (1985): 295–310.

Voci, Anna Maria. *Petrarca e la vita religiosa: Il mito umanista della vita eremitica*. Rome: Istituto storico italiano per l'età moderna e contemporanea, 1983.

Wheeler, Arthur Leslie. *Ovid with an English Translation: Tristia, Ex Ponto*. Vol. 10. Cambridge, MA: Harvard University Press, 1965.

Wilkins, Ernest H. "Petrarch's Coronation Oration." *PMLA* 68.5 (1953): 1241–50.

———. "Petrarch's Ecclesiastical Career." *Speculum* 28.4 (1953): 754–75.

Witke, Charles. *Numen Litterarum: The Old and the New in Latin Poetry from Constantine to Gregory the Great*. Leiden: Brill, 1971.

Witt, Ronald G. *In the Footsteps of the Ancients: The Origins of Humanism from Lovato to Bruni*. Leiden: Brill, 2000.

———. "Petrarch, Creator of the Christian Humanist." In *Petrarch and Boccaccio: The Unity of Knowledge in the Pre-Modern World*, ed. Igor Candido, 65–77. Berlin: De Gruyter, 2018.

Yocum, Demetrio S. *Petrarch's Humanist Writing and Carthusian Monasticism: The Secret Language of the Self*. Turnhout: Brepols, 2013.

INDEX OF REFERENCES AND PASSAGES FROM PETRARCH'S WORKS

Africa, xxv, xlvn25
  2.347–50, 30n43, 45n111
  5.402–4, 40n86
  5.403–4, 25n21
  7.673–74, 44n103
Bucolicum carmen, xxiv, xlivn21
  Parthenias (1st eclogue), xxiv–xxv,
    xxxiii, xxxvii–xxxviii, xl, xlivn21,
    xlvn25, xlvin27, xlixn44, livn82,
    lviinn93–94, 20n5, 36n69
  Pietas pastoralis (5th eclogue),
    xlviin28
  Divortium (8th eclogue), 26n25
  Querulus (9th eclogue), 25n21,
    40n83
  Laurea occidens (10th eclogue),
    xxvi–xxvii, lin54
  Galathea (11th eclogue), 23n14
De otio religioso (*Dor.*)., xix, xxii, xxiii,
  xlivn18, xlvn25, 25n20, 26n22,
  26n25, 27n28, 31n44, 36n70,
  37.75, 39n82, 45n110, 47n115
De remediis, 20n7, 30n43, 34n61,
  36n68, 38n78, 40n83
De sui ipsius, 29n38, 36n67, 44n105
De viris illustribus, lviin98
De vita solitaria (*Dvs.*), xix, xxii, xxiii,
  xxviii, xxxii, xlvn25, liiin76,
  21n10, 23n14, 24n19, 27n28,
  31n46, 37n75, 39n82, 43n98
Epistulae metricae, 20n4, 21n12,
  25n21, 26n25, 27n28, 30n41,
  31n46, 40n83, 45n111
Familiares (*Fam.*)
  1.2, 45n111
  1.3, 30n43
  1.7, 34n60
  2.1, 38n80
  2.4, 24n15
  2.9, 26n23, 27n28, 32n50, 36n70
  4.1, xlviin32
  4.12, 30n41, 48n117
  5.1, 32n47
  5.5, liiin77, lixn102
  5.18, 24n19, 26n25, 48n117
  7.3, xliiin10
  7.9, 20n7
  7.12, 40n86
  7.17, 23n14, 43n97, 43n101
  8.3, 32n47, 35n63
  9.1, 29n37
  9.13, 65n28
  10.1, 30n43
  10.2, 22n13
  10.3, xliiin16, xlviinn30–31, xlvin33,
    22n13, 26n25, 34n61, 35n64,
    45n110
  10.4, xx, xxiv–xxv, xxvi, xxxvii,
    xlivn22, xlvn25, xlvin27, xlixn41,
    xlixnn43–44, lin53, liiin70, liiin77,
    lviin92, lviin96
  10.5, xliiin10, livn81, 28n32, 42n92

11.3, 45n111
12.3, 23n14
12.14, 42n91
12.15, 64n21
15.8, 33n57
15.11, 32n47, 32n49
15.12, 32n47
15.4, 29n39
16.4, 37n76
17.1, 22n13
17.10, 44n104
19.12, 32n49
19.16, 30n40, 39n82
20.1, 39n82
20.2, 46n112
20.8, 29n37
22.10, xxviii, xl, xliiin14, xlivn21, lin59, lixn103
23.2, 30n43
23.12, 29n37, 32n50
24.1, 30n43, 43n102
*Invective*s, xlin3
Itinerarium, lixn102, 63n18
Liber sine nomine, 42n95
Memoriale, xxxiii, xlvn25
Rerum memorandarum libri, 38n78, 45n111
Rerum vulgarium fragmenta (*Rvf*.), xx, xxviii–xxix, lin50, lvn87
  1.10, 47n114
  15.2, 38n80
  23.25, 28n33
  25.5, 33n55
  26.2, 21n12
  39.8, 28n33
  55.15, 25n21
  59.4, 25n21
  62.7–8, 25n21
  62.12, 27n27
  68, 20n3
  76.6–8, 25n20
  80, 21n12
  80.36, 26n25
  81.1, 24n19, 38n80
  81.3, 41n88
  89.10, 25n21
  96.4, 25n21
  96.9–10, 25n20
  97.1, 25n20
  106.5, 25n21
  128.117, 24n19
  128.97–99, 30n43
  133.2–3, 45n111
  151.1–2, 21n12
  181.1, 25n21
  189, 21n12
  197.3, 24n19
  205.2, 24n19
  211.2, 26n25
  216.1–4, 29n39
  226.8, 29n39
  234.1, 29n39
  235.5, 21n12
  264.111–12, 24n16
  264.12–13, 41n88
  264.127, 27n30
  264.136, 44n104
  272.1, 30n43
  294.12, 45n111
  319.1–2, 45n111
  331.22, 45n111
  365.14, 38n77
  366.111–12, 28n33
  366.69–70, 21n12
  366.120, 27n27
Secretum, xxii, xxiii, xxx, 20n7, 21n10, 21n12, 23n14, 24n16, 24nn18–19, 26n25, 27n28, 30n41, 31n44, 31n46, 32nn49–50, 36n70, 37n76, 38n77, 38n80, 40n86, 42n92, 45n109, 47n114, 63n13

Seniles (Sen.)
　1.5, ln48, 45n111
　1.7, 26n24
　3.1, 20n7
　10.1, xxiii, xxxviii, xlviiin37, liin62, lviin98, lviiin99, 38n77
　10.2, lixn101, 65n29
　15.5, xvii, xviii, xlin1–2, xliiin15
　15.15, xlivn23
Testamentum, xxvii, xlin4
Triumphus Aeternitatis, 45n111

INDEX OF SCRIPTURAL REFERENCES

Old Testament

Ecclesiastes (Qoheleth) 6.9, 45n108
Ecclesiasticus (Sirach)
  5.5, 28n31
  14.18–19, 47n116
  37.3, 45n108
Exodus (Ex.) 34.8, 41n88
Ezechiel (Ez.)
  11.19, 62n2
  37.12–13, 27n30
Genesis (Gn.)
  2.7, 45n111
  3.19, 45n111
  17.3, 41n88
Isaiah (Is.)
  42.14, 42n94
  45.16, 34n59
  52.13–53.12, 47n114
  54.4, 34n59
Jeremiah (Jer.) 20.7, 47n114
Job
  4.13–14, 38n78
  7.14, 38n78
  7.5, 42n92
  7.9–10, 62n4
  7.14, 38n78
  8.9, 45n111
  9.18, 38n79
  9.25, 30n42
  10.1, 38n79

  13.28, 42n92
  14.2, 45n111
  17.1, 31nn44–45
  17.13, 21n8
  25.6, 42n92
  33.28, 21n9
  33.19, 29n39
  34.21, 37n73
Joshua 5.15, 41n88
Lamentations (Lam.)
  3.14, 47n114
  3.15, 38n79
  3.27, 24n19
Micah 7.6, 39n81
Numbers (Nm.), 16.4, 41n88
Proverbs (Prv.)
  4.19, 43n97
  5.22, 25n21
  24.11, 21n9
  26.11, 44n105
Psalms (Ps.)
  2.4, 26n24
  2.11, 45n110
  4.5, 24n17
  5.7 (5.6), 47n116
  6, lvn90
  6.7, 29n39
  7.2 (7.1), 43n96
  8.4 (8.3), 35n62

Psalms (Ps.) (*cont.*)
  8.6–7 (8.5), 35n66
  8.7 (8.6), 35n64
  9.19 (9.18), 42n95
  12.2 (13.2), 30n43
  12.4 (13.3), 21n9, 62n5
  12.6 (13.5), 40n84
  13.2 (14.2), 42n93
  15.7 (16.7), 32n48
  15.11 (16.11), 36n70
  16.8 (17.8), 47n113
  16.9–11 (17.9), 40n86
  17.18 (18.17), 32n50
  17.43 (18.42), 45n111
  21.8 (22.7), 47n114
  21.12 (22.11), 33n52
  24.2 (25.2), 27n29
  24.4 (25.4), 33n55
  24.7 (25.7), xix
  26.5 (27.5), 37n71
  26.9 (27.9), 62n5
  26.11 (27.11), 33n55
  29.6 (30.5), 29n36
  30.3 (31.2), 40n85
  30.16 (31.15), 32n50
  32.13 (33.13), 34n58
  34.5 (35.5), 45n111
  36.13 (37.13), 26n24
  37 (38), xxxii, xxxiv, lvn90
  37.6 (38.5), 42n92
  37.7 (38.6), 38n80
  39.3 (40.2), 36n70, 48n117
  41.4 (42.4), 20n7
  42.1, 28n34
  43.16 (44.15), 34n59
  43.20 (44.19), 41n87
  45.11 (46.10), xix, 25n20
  50 (51), xxxi, xxxii, xxxiii,
    xxxiv–xxxv, xlvn25, lvn90, 20n1,
    27n27, 63n14
  50.1 (51.1), xlvn25, lvn90
  50.3 (51.2), 27n27, 63n14
  50.12 (51.11), 62n6
  50.16 (51.14), 47n116
  54.5–6 (55.4–5), 41n87
  54.6 (55.5), 45n110
  54.24, 47n116
  55.3 (56.2), 40n86, 41n89
  56.2 (57.1), 27n27
  56.7 (57.6), 25n21
  58.2 (59.2), 32n50
  58.3 (59.2), 47n116
  62.8 (63.7), 47n113
  68.3 (69.2), 21n12, 30n41
  68.7 (69.6), 34n59
  68.8, and 20 (69.7, and 19), 34n59
  68.12 (69.11), 47n114
  68.15, 48n117
  69 (70), xliiin11
  70.3 (71.3), 41n88
  73.16–17 (74.16–17), 34n61
  73.19 (74.19), 42n95
  77.33 (78.33), 30n42
  79.14 (80.13), 20n6, 28n34
  90.5 (91.5), 38n78
  101 (102), xxxii, xxxiv, lvi
  101.4, 12 (102.3, 11), 30n42,
    45n111
  101.7 (102.6), xlin3
  102 (103), xxxiv
  102.14, 45n111
  103.6–9 (104.6–9), 64n24
  103.19–20 (104.19–20), 34n61
  106.12 (107.12), 33n52
  106.26 (107.26), 30n41
  113.8 (114.8), 28n33
  118.34, and 125 (119.34, and 125),
    32n48
  118.35 (119.35), 62n5
  118.61 (119.61), 25n21
  118.133 (119.133), 36n70, 62n50
  118.164 (119.164), xxxiii

Index of Scriptural References   85

123.7 (124.7), 25n21
123.8 (124.8), xxii, xlviin33
129 (130), xxxii, xxxiv
137.8 (138.8), 33n51, 63n14
138.8 (139.8), 64n23
142 (143), xxxii, xxxiv, lvn90
142.3 (143.3), 40n86
142.7 (143.7), 62n5
142.8 (143.8), 36n70
142.9 (143.9), 32n50

142.10 (143.10), 32n49
143.4 (144.4), 45n111
Song of Songs (Cant.)
  1.15, 29n39
  3.1, 29n39
  5.7, 39n82
Wisdom (Wis.)
  2.5, 45n111
  5.9 and 15, 45n111

New Testament

John (Jn.)
  1.13, 47n116
  11.1–44, 27n30
Luke (Lk.)
  6.35, 38n77
  7.11–17, 27n30
  8.22, 64n25
  8.25, 64n24
  10.27, 62n7
  10.30, 41n90
  24.29, 33n56
  24.13–35, 37n72
Mark (Mk.)
  4.37–39, 64n25
  5.21–43, 27n30
  13.30, 62n7
Matthew (Mt.)
  6.34, 31n46
  10.36, 39n81
  11.5, 27n30
  11.30, 24n19
  14.28–32, 64n25
  22.37, 62n7
  24.51, 31n45
  25.30, 31n45

Paul, St.
  1 Corinthians
  —2.3, 45n110
  —4.7, 37n76
  —10.12, 41n88
  Ephesians, 6.5, 45n110
  Galatians
  —5.1, 24n19
  —6.3, 44n106
  Philippians, 2.12, 45n110
  Romans 7.15 and 20, 44n104
2 Peter (Pet.)
  1.19, 45n107
  2.22, 28n34

GENERAL INDEX

A
Agatha, St., 57, 63n18, 64n19
Alighieri, Dante
   and David, xxx–xxxi
   and the *Commedia*, xxx–xxxi, 63n16
   in *Parthenias*, xlixn44
   and Petrarch, xxix, xxx–xxxi, xlivn21, xlixn44
   and Psalm 50, xxxi
   and St. Laurence, 63n16
   on the translation of the Psalms, xlixn42
Ambrose, St.
   and hymnody, xxviii
   influence on Petrarch, xxvi, xxix–xxx, xlivn21
   on St. Laurence, 63n16
Aquinas, Thomas, 28n32, 33n53, 62n7
Arator, xxvii
Archpoet, the, 38n79
Ascoli, Albert, xlixn44
Augustine, St.
   and Ambrose, xxix–xxx
   classical influence on, ln46
   Confessions, xxiii, xxix–xxx, ln46, 24n17, 26n25, 45n111
   on conversion of sinners, 33n53
   De civitate dei 4.3, 47n116
   vs. Donatists, xxx
   Enarrationes in Psalmos, 24n17, 48n117

Evangelium Johannis Tractatus, 45n111
   influence on Petrarch, xxi, xxiii, xxv–xxvi, xxix–xxx, xxxix, xlivn21, 43n102, 48n117, 62n1
   Psalmus contra partem Donati, xxx
   and scripture, ln46
   Sermo 235.2, 37n72
   and seven penitential Psalms, xxix, livn79
   Soliloquia 1, 41n88

B
Barański, Zygmunt, xlixn44
Bartolomeo da Urbino, xxx
Benedict, St., *Rule* of, xxxiii
Benedictine order
   liturgy of, xxvii
   and Petrarch's psalms, xliii
Bible, the
   editions of, xxiv
   versification of, xxvi
   See also Divine Office; Psalms, biblical book of; scripture
Boccaccio, Giovanni, 63n16
books of hours. *See* Divine Office, Psalms, biblical book of
breviaries
   of Petrarch, xvii, xviii, xxiv, xxviii, xxxi–xxxii, xlin4, xlviiin39
   types of, xxxi

breviaries (*cont.*)
  See also devotion; Divine Office;
    Petrarch; Psalms, biblical book of
Bruni, Francesco, xxii, 33n54

C
Cachey, Theodore J., Jr, 21n12, 22n13
Carmina Burana, 38n79, 41n88,
  45n111
Carthusian order
  and Berengar of Poitiers, xlvn25
  and *devotio moderna*, xxviii
  and Gherardo, xvii, xxv, 22n13
  at Montrieux, xvii
  Petrarch's relationship to, xix, xxii,
    xxix, xlvin27, xlviin35
Casali, Marino, xlvn25, 20n7
Cassian, xxxiii, xxxvi–xxxvii, xliiin11,
  livn83
Cassiodorus, xxix, xxxii, xxxix, lvn84
Catullus, 40n83
Chapman, George, ln50
Christianity
  and church fathers,
    xxvi, xxxvi–xxxvii
  and early Latin poets, xxvi, xxviii
  vs. heresies, xlixn44
  and hymnody, xix, xxvii
  and *lectio divina*, xix, xxxii
  and the liturgy, xviii, xix, xxvi, xxvii,
    xxviii, xxxi–xxxii, xxxiii, xliiin11,
    65n29
  Petrarch's view of, xx–xxi, xxv–xxvi,
    xxvii, ln48
  and popular devotion, xxix,
    xxxi–xxxii
  and prayer, xxxix, 65n29
  and psalmody, xxxvi–xxxvii, 65n29
  and sin, lvn84
church, the
  doctrine of, xx–xxi

  liturgy of, xviii, xxxi, xxxiii,
    xxxi–xxxii, xxxiii
  and Petrarch, xx–xxi, xxviii
  See also devotion; Petrarch
Cicero, xxvii, ln46, 36n67–69, 42n91
Cochin, Henry, 27n26, 47n116
Cola di Rienzo
  failed coup of, xx, xxii
  Petrarch's support of, xvii, xlin5,
    xlviin28
Colonna family, xlin5, xlvin26, lixn102
Coppini, Donatella, xlviin35, 21n11,
  62n1, 62n12, 64n22, 64n26
cursus, lviin98. *See also* psalms, of
  Petrarch

D
David, king
  as Christian poet, xxiv, xxix, xlixn44
  and Dante, xxx–xxxi
  and humility, xxxvi
  and Petrarch, xviii–xix, xxviii, xxix,
    xxxi, xl, xlivn21, xlvn25, 20n7
  as penitent sinner, xxviii
  and the Psalms, xviii–xix, xx, xxiii,
    xxiv, xxv, xxxi, xxxiii, xlivn21
  voice of, xx, xxv, xxxvii, xlivn22,
    xlvn25
devotio moderna, xxviii
devotion
  Christian, xviii, xix, xxviii, xxix
  and Petrarch's psalms, xxii, xxiii, xxvi,
    xxviii, xl, xlviiin36
  See also Christianity; Petrarch;
    prayers, of Petrarch; Psalms, bibli-
    cal book of; psalms, of Petrarch
Divine Office
  and books of hours, xviii, xxviii,
    xliiin11, 65n29
  and Cassian, xliiin11
  and the *Gloria Patri*, xxxiii, livn83

and hymnody, xxvii
origins of, xix, xxxii
and psalmody, xxxvi–xxxvii, 65n29
recitation of, xvii, xviii, xix, xxv, xxxi, 61, 65n29, xliiinn10–11, lvn84, 65n29
and types of breviaries, xxviii, xxxi–xxxii
See also Petrarch; prayers, of Petrarch; Psalms, biblical book of; psalms, of Petrarch

E
Erasmus, St., 59, 64n26
Eusebius of Cremona, 62n10

F
Francis, St.
   Canticle of, xxxi, lvn88
   and the *Office of the Passion*, xxxii, liiin71, liiin75
   as Petrarch's model, xxx, xxxi–xxxii
   and scripture, xxxi
   and solitude, xxxii
Franciscan order
   and breviaries, xxxi–xxxii
   and Petrarch, liiin77

G
Geri, Lorenzo, xlviin35
Gherardo
   as a Carthusian, xvii, xxii, xxv
   and Dante, xlixn44
   as Monicus in *Parthenias*, xxv, xxxvii–xxxviii, xlixn44
   and Petrarch, xvii, xviii–xix, xxii, xxiv, xxv, xxxii–xxxiii, xxxvii–xxxviii, xlvn25, xlvin27, xlviin33, xlixn44, 22n13
Gigliucci, Roberto, 29n37, 45n111
Giovanni da Bocheta, xlin4

Giovanni Mandelli, lixn102
Gloria Patri, xxxiii, livn83
Graves, Michael, xlviiin39
Gregory the Great, xlivn21, 48n117
Guido Faba, lviin98

H
Hankins, James, xlin5
heu, xxx, xxxiii, xxxv, xlvn25, lvn90, 2, 20n1, 29n37, 40n86, 42n92, 50
Holy Land, the, 63n18
Homer, xxv, xxxvii, xl, xlivn21
Horace, xxvii, lvn89, 30n43, 31n46, 45n111, 47n114
Hortis, Attilio, 63n18
hymnody, xix, xxvii, xxviii, xxix, liin67

J
Jerome, St.
   classical training of, xxiv, ln46
   Epistle 106, xlviiin39, lxi
   and Hebrew Psalter, lviin97
   influence on Petrarch, xix, xxiv–xxv, xxv–xxvi, xxxvii, xxxviii, xlivn21
   letter to Eustochium, ln46
   as translator of the Psalms, xxiv–xxv, xlviiin39, xlixn40, lviin92
Jesus Christ
   Incarnation of, xxxix
   invocation to, 19, 27n28, 40n85, 51, 53, 55, 57, 59, 61
   Passion of, 47n114
   resurrection of the dead, 27n30
   yoke of, 24n19
Juvenal, 63n13

L
Lactantius, 23n14
Laurence, St., 57, 63n16–17
lectio divina, xix, xxxii
liturgy of the hours. *See* Divine Office

Ludolph of Saxony, xlviin35
Ludwig van Kempen, xliiin10
Lummus, David, xlixn44

M
Martellotti, Guido, xlivn21, xlvn25
Martinez, Ronald, xlviin33, lvn90
Mary, mother of God, xxvii, xlviiin36, liiin75, 57, 61
Matter, E. Ann, lvn90
Milan, xxviii, xxix
Miserere. See Psalm 50 (51)

N
Naples, liiin77
Nelli, Francesco, xviii, xxviii, xlivn21
Nicholas, St., 59, 64n26, 65n27
Nicholas III, pope, xxxi
Nolhac, Pierre de, xlvn25

O
Opus Dei. See Divine Office
Oratio contra tempestates, xxxix, xl, 63n15, 63n18. *See also* Petrarch; prayers, of Petrarch; psalms, of Petrarch
Orationes quotidianae, xxxix, 28n33, 36n70, 37n74, 39n80, 40n85, 63n18. *See also* Petrarch; prayers, of Petrarch; psalms, of Petrarch
Origen
 the Hexaplaric Septuagint, xxiv
Orpheus, myth of, xlixn44
Ovid, xxvii, lvn89, 20n7, 30n43, 36n68, 44n104, 47n114

P
Paul, St., xlivn21
Petrarch
 and Ambrose, xxvi, xxix–xxx, xlivn21
 and Augustine, xxi, xxiii, xxv–xxvi, xxix–xxx, xxxix, xlivn21, 43n102, 48n117, 62n1
 breviaries of, xvii, xviii, xxiv, xxviii, xxxi–xxxii, xlin4, xlviiin39
 and the Carthusians, xix, xxii, xxix, xlvin27, xlviin35
 Christian humanism of, xx–xxi, xxiii, xxv–xxvi, xxvii, xxxv, xxxviii, xlixn44, ln48, 32n50, 33n57
 and the church, xx–xxi, xxviii, ln48
 on the church fathers, ln48
 and classical culture, xxi, xxv–xxvi, xxvii, xl, xlivn21, ln48, 32n50
 as a cleric, xviii, xxxvii, xxxviii–xxxix, xlviin33
 and Cola di Rienzo, xvii, xlin5, xlviin28
 on concupiscence, 25n20
 and courtly love, 24n19
 and Dante, xxix, xxx–xxxi, xlivn21, xlixn44
 and David, xviii–xix, xxviii, xxix, xxxi, xl, xlivn21, xlvn25, 20n7
 on death, xviii, xlin4, 31n44, 64n22
 and the Divine Office, xvii, xviii, xix, xxv, xxxii–xxxiii, xxxix, xliiin10, 65n29
 and Franciscans, liiin77
 and Francis of Assisi, xxx, xxxi–xxxii
 and Gherardo, xvii, xviii–xix, xxii, xxiv, xxv, xxxii–xxxiii, xxxvii–xxxviii, xlvn25, xlvin27, xlviin33, xlixn44, 22n13
 and God's mercy, xix, 26n23, 37n75, 38n77
 hope in, 29n38, 30n40, 38n77, 39n82, 40n83, 40n86
 and *imago Dei*, xxxv, 34n61
 and Jerome, xix, xxiv–xxv, xxv–xxvi, xxxvii, xxxviii, xlivn21

and the lauda tradition, liiin72
and Laura, xxii
life of, xvii, xix, xxi–xxii, xxv, liiin77, lixn102, 20n4, 43n102
and lust, xxxiii, xxxviii, xlvn25, livn81
and monasticism, xvii, xxi, xxii, xxv, xxxvi, xxxvii, xlviin33
monastic style in, xix, xx, xxii, 22n13
and Mount Ventoux, xxii
and MS Paris Latin 2201, 62n12, 63n15
and MS Paris Latin 2923, xlvn25
in Naples, liiin77
and old age, 26n25
and patristic literature, xxi, 32n50
poetics of, xxxviii
as poet laureate, xvii–xviii, xxi
and poetry, xxxiv–xxv
politics of, xx, xxi, xxii
and posterity, xxi
and prayer, xxix, xxxix–xl, xliiin10
and the Psalms, xviii–xix, xx, xxiii, xxiv–xxv, xxix, xxxvii–xxxviii, xlin3, xlivn22, xlvn25, lin60
relationship to God, xvii, xviii, xx, xxiii, xxx, xxxviii
as religious writer, xx, xxi, xxii–xxiii, xlixn44
and salvation, xxvi, xxvii
and scripture, xix, xxix, xlviiin39
and sea-related imagery, xxxix–xl, liiin77, lixn102, 22n13, 63n18
and sin, xix, xxiii, xxx
as Silvius in *Parthenias*, xxv, xxxvii–xxxviii, xlvn25, xlvin27, xlixn44
snare-related imagery in, 25n21
soul in, 22n13, 25n20, 26n25, 28n33, 34n61, 39n82
testament of, xvii, xlin4

and theology, xxiv–xxv
and Vaucluse, xix, xxi
and weakness, 32n49
on women, livn81
and youth, 26n25
See also prayers, of Petrarch; Psalms, biblical book of; psalms, of Petrarch
pia dictamina, xxvii. *See also* hymnody
Pier Damiani, 42n91
Pliny, the Elder, 44n106
Pozzi, Giovanni, xxxvii, lvn90
prayers, of Petrarch
authorship of, xxxix
body in, 51, 55, 62n1, 62n12
danger in, 57, 59, 64n22
darkness in, 53
death in, 51, 53, 55, 57, 59, 61, 63n13, 63n18, 64n22
earth in, 57, 59
enemies in, 51, 53, 55
fear in, 55, 59, 63n18, 64n22
God's help in, 55, 57, 59, 61
God's mercy in, 53, 55, 57, 59
the heart in, 51, 53, 55, 62n7
heaven in, 51, 57, 59, 61
hope in, 51, 57, 59,
iniquities in, 51, 53, 55
intercession in, 57, 59, 61, 63n17
invocation to God in, 51, 53, 55, 63n14
liturgical seasons in, 65n29
lust in, 53
manuscript tradition of, xxxix
miseria in, 38n80, 53, 55, 63n14, 64n20, 65n27
mockery in, 17, 47n114
and Petrarch's psalms, xxxix
salvation in, 36n70, 51, 53, 55, 61
sea-related imagery in, xxxix–xl, 59, 61, 63n18

prayers, of Petrarch (*cont.*)
  sin in, 55, 57, 62n1
  soul in, xxxix, 51, 53, 55, 57, 59, 62n1
  See also Petrarch; Psalms, biblical book of; Psalms, of Petrarch
Prosper of Aquitaine, xxvi–xxvii
Prudentius, xxvi–xxvii
Psalm 50 (51), xxxi, xxxii, xxxiii, xxxiv–xxxv, xlvn25, lvn90, 20n1, 27n27, 63n14
Psalms, biblical book of
  and Augustine, xxix
  and books of prayers, xxvi, xxviii
  and Cassiodorus, xxix
  and the Gallican Psalter, xxiv, xlviiin39, lviin97
  and the *Gloria Patri*, xxxiii, livn83
  God's help in, xxii
  God's mercy in, xxxiv, 27n27, lvn90, 63n14
  and Hebrew Psalter, lviin97
  influence on *Rvf.*, lin60
  and Jerome, xxiv, xxxvii, xxxviii, xlviiin39, xlixn42, lviin92, lviin97
  in the Jewish tradition, xviii
  and the number seven, lvn84
  and penitential dimension of, xxix, xxxiii–xxxiv, lvn84
  Petrarch's familiarity with, xviii–xix, xxiv–xxv, xlin3, lin60
  vs. Petrarch's psalms, xxviii–xxix, xxxii–xxxiv
  poetic style of, xxxvii–xxxviii, xlivn22, lviin92
  as poetry, xx, xxiii, xxiv–xxv, xlivn21, xlivn22, xlixn42
  and popular devotion, xviii, xxvi, xxix, xxx, xxxii
  recitation of, xix, xxiii, xxv, xxix–xxx, xxxi, xxxii–xxxiii, xxxvi–xxxvii
  and sin, xix, lvn84
  and the Septuagint, lviin97
  and the seven penitential Psalms, xxix, xxxii–xxxiv, xxxviii, lvn90
  translations of, xlixn42
  the *Vetus Latina* version of, xxiv
  and the Vulgate Psalter, xxiv
  See also Petrarch; prayers, of Petrarch
psalms, of Petrarch
  acedia in, xxxviii, 20n7
  amaritudo animae in, 38n79
  Augustine's influence on, xxix–xxx
  beauty of creation in, 11, 34n61
  bed imagery in, 29n39
  circulation of, xxiii, xxix, xlviin35, xlviiin36
  classical influences on, xx, xxiii, xxv, xxvii, lvn89, 47n114
  danger in, 3, 5, 7, 17, 21n12, 23n14
  darkness in, 5, 9, 13, 40n86
  dating of, xxi, xlvn25, xlixn44, 62n12
  and David, xx, xxiii, xxiv, xxviii, xxix, xxxiv, xxxvi, xxxvii, xxxviii, xl, xlivn21, xlvn25, xlixn44, lixn103, 20n7
  death in, 5, 7, 13, 15, 23n14, 25n21, 30n43, 40n85, 40n86, 42n92
  description of, xxiii–xxiv
  earth in, 11, 34n61
  Emmaus episode in, 37n72
  enemies in, xxxiv, xxxv, 3, 5, 7, 9, 13, 27n28, 31n44, 32n50, 39n82, 40n85, 41n89, 47n116
  eyes in, 5, 7, 9, 13, 21n9, 22n13, 31n44, 37n73
  fear in, 3, 5, 7, 15, 17, 22n13, 27n30, 41n87, 42n92, 45n110, 47n116
  and Francis's *Canticle*, xxxiv–xxxv, lvn88
  the *Gloria Patri* in, xxxiii, xlviin34
  God's gifts in, 34n61, 35n65

God's help in, xxxiv, lvn88, 5, 13, 15, 27n28
God's mercy in, xxxiv, xxxv, xxxvi, xxxviii, lvi, 5, 7, 9, 11, 13, 15, 19, 29n35, 33n53
God's mockery in, 5
the heart in, 9, 15, 25n20, 27n30, 28n33, 32n47, 41n87, 44n106, 45n108
heaven in, 5, 11, 20n3, 26n24, 34n58, 34n61, 35n62, 36n68, 42n93
hope in, xxxv, xxxvi, xxxviii, 3, 5, 7, 11, 13, 15
the human body in, 7, 11, 13, 38n80
humility in, xxxvi
imago Dei in, xxxv, 34n61
influence of, ln50
ingratitudo in, 38n77
invocation to God, xlviin34, lvn90, 27n27
vs. Jerome's Latin translation, xxxvii, xxxviii, lviin92
and Job, 21n8, 29n39, 30n42, 31n44, 37n73, 38n78, 42n92, 45n111, 62n4
as literary model, xxvi
and lust in, xxxiii, xxxviii, xlvn25, 19, 25n20, 48n117
and manuscript tradition, xlviin35
miseria in, xxiii, xxiv, xxx, xxix, xxxiii–xxxiv, xxxv–xxxvi, xxxviii, xlvn25, 3, 7, 9, 40n86, 42n92, 48n117
penitential tone of, xxxiii–xxxv, xxxvi
and Petrarch's prayers, xxxix
and popular devotion, xlviiin36
praise in, xxxiv–xxxv
psalm 4, xxxiv–xxxv, lvn88
recitation of, xlviiin36
and *Rvf.*, xxviii–xxix, lvn87
salvation in, xxxiv, xxxv, xxxvii, lvn87, 3, 5, 7, 13, 40n83
sea-related imagery in, xl, 3, 9, 11, 21n12, 34n61, 43n98
and the self, xxviii, xxx, xxxv, xxxviii, lvn87
sequence of, xxxiv–xxxvi, lvn90
vs. the seven penitential Psalms, lvn90
and sin, xxxiv, xxxv, 3, 5, 7, 24n17, 25n20, 26n25, 28n32, 29n35, 33n53, 34n61, 38n80, 42n92, 43n102, 45n109
soul in, xxxiv, xxxviii, 3, 7, 9, 13, 17, 21n9, 29n35
style of, xx, xxii, xxiii–xxiv, xxv, xxxvii–xxxviii, lvn88, lviin98
themes in, xxxiii–xxxv, lvn90
time in, 30n43
title of, xlviiin38
toil in, 3, 9, 11
vs. the traditional Psalms, xxviii, xxxiii–xxxiv, xxxviii, lvn90
trust in God, 17
use of the *cursus* in, xxxviii, lvn88, lviin98
See also Petrarch; prayers, of Petrarch; Psalms, biblical book of
Pythagoras, 23n14

R
Rauner, Erwin, xlviin35, 64n26
Rico, Francisco, 20n7, 28n33, 62n1

S
Sagremor de Pommiers, xxiii, xxxiii, xxxviii
scripture
and Petrarch, xix, xxix, xlin3
rewritings of, xxvi
style of, xxv

scripture (*cont.*)
  See also Divine Office; Psalms, biblical book of
Sedulius, xxxvi–xxvii, 28n34, 30n40
Seneca, 20n7, 30n43, 31n46, 32n47, 46n112
Statius, 42n92

T

tears, xx, xxix–xxx, xxxvii, xxxviii, xlivn22, 7, 17, 20n7, 28n33, 29n39, 51, 62n10

V

Virgil, xx, xxv, xxxvii, xl, xlivn21, xlixn44, 30n43, 32n50, 48n118

FRANCESCO PETRARCA
(1304–1374) was a scholar and poet of early Renaissance Italy. He is widely recognized as the "Father of Humanism," emphasizing the study of authors and thinkers from classical antiquity through the Middle Ages.

DEMETRIO S. YOCUM
is senior research associate for the Notre Dame Center for Italian Studies.